HBR Guide to
AI Basics for Managers

Harvard Business Review Guides

Arm yourself with the advice you need to succeed on the job, from the most trusted brand in business. Packed with how-to essentials from leading experts, the HBR Guides provide smart answers to your most pressing work challenges.

The titles include:

HBR Guide for Women at Work
HBR Guide to AI Basics for Managers
HBR Guide to Being a Great Boss
HBR Guide to Being More Productive
HBR Guide to Better Business Writing
HBR Guide to Better Mental Health at Work
HBR Guide to Building Your Business Case
HBR Guide to Buying a Small Business
HBR Guide to Changing Your Career
HBR Guide to Coaching Employees
HBR Guide to Collaborative Teams
HBR Guide to Critical Thinking
HBR Guide to Data Analytics Basics for Managers
HBR Guide to Dealing with Conflict
HBR Guide to Delivering Effective Feedback
HBR Guide to Emotional Intelligence
HBR Guide to Finance Basics for Managers
HBR Guide to Getting the Mentoring You Need
HBR Guide to Getting the Right Job

HBR Guide to Getting the Right Work Done

HBR Guide to Leading Teams

HBR Guide to Making Better Decisions

HBR Guide to Making Every Meeting Matter

HBR Guide to Managing Flexible Work

HBR Guide to Managing Strategic Initiatives

HBR Guide to Managing Stress at Work

HBR Guide to Managing Up and Across

HBR Guide to Motivating People

HBR Guide to Negotiating

HBR Guide to Networking

HBR Guide to Office Politics

HBR Guide to Performance Management

HBR Guide to Persuasive Presentations

HBR Guide to Project Management

HBR Guide to Remote Work

HBR Guide to Setting Your Strategy

HBR Guide to Smarter Networking

HBR Guide to Thinking Strategically

HBR Guide to Work-Life Balance

HBR Guide to Your Professional Growth

HBR Guide to **AI Basics for Managers**

HARVARD BUSINESS REVIEW PRESS

Boston, Massachusetts

HBR Press Quantity Sales Discounts

Harvard Business Review Press titles are available at significant quantity discounts when purchased in bulk for client gifts, sales promotions, and premiums. Special editions, including books with corporate logos, customized covers, and letters from the company or CEO printed in the front matter, as well as excerpts of existing books, can also be created in large quantities for special needs.

For details and discount information for both print and ebook formats, contact booksales@harvardbusiness.org, tel. 800-988-0886, or www.hbr.org/bulksales.

Copyright 2023 Harvard Business School Publishing Corporation

All rights reserved

Printed in the United States of America

10 9 8 7 6 5 4 3 2 1

No part of this publication may be reproduced, stored in, or introduced into a retrieval system, or transmitted, in any form, or by any means (electronic, mechanical, photocopying, recording, or otherwise), without the prior permission of the publisher. Requests for permission should be directed to permissions@harvardbusiness.org, or mailed to Permissions, Harvard Business School Publishing, 60 Harvard Way, Boston, Massachusetts 02163.

The web addresses referenced in this book were live and correct at the time of the book's publication but may be subject to change.

Library of Congress Cataloging-in-Publication Data

Names: Harvard Business Review Press, issuing body.
Title: HBR guide to AI basics for managers / Harvard Business Review.
Other titles: Harvard business review guide to AI basics for managers | Harvard business review guides.
Description: Boston, Massachusetts : Harvard Business Review Press, [2023] | Series: HBR guides | Includes index.
Identifiers: LCCN 2022030290 (print) | LCCN 2022030291 (ebook) | ISBN 9781647824433 (paperback) | ISBN 9781647824440 (epub)
Subjects: LCSH: Artificial intelligence. | Management—Technological innovations. | Business enterprises—Information technology—Management. | Industrial management. | Success in business.
Classification: LCC HD30.2 .H325 2023 (print) | LCC HD30.2 (ebook) | DDC 658.4/038—dc23/eng/20220907
LC record available at https://lccn.loc.gov/2022030290
LC ebook record available at https://lccn.loc.gov/2022030291

ISBN: 978-1-64782-443-3
eISBN: 978-1-64782-444-0

The paper used in this publication meets the requirements of the American National Standard for Permanence of Paper for Publications and Documents in Libraries and Archives Z39.48-1992.

What You'll Learn

Artificial Intelligence (AI) is having a transformational impact on business. From product design and financial modeling to performance management and marketing spending, AI and machine learning are becoming everyday tools for managers in organizations of all sizes. You can't just leave AI to the experts anymore. If you don't understand the technology at a foundational level, you're not going to be informed enough to make smart decisions that will affect your bottom line. And if you don't realize how AI will change jobs—including the work that managers and leaders do—you may make a major misstep in your career.

Whether you want to get up to speed quickly, could use a refresher, or are working with an AI expert for the first time, the *HBR Guide to AI Basics for Managers* will provide you with the information and skills you need. With practical, applicable advice and plain-language takeaways in each chapter, the book will help you take the first steps toward embracing AI and transforming your business.

What You'll Learn

You'll learn how to:

- Understand key terms and concepts, including machine learning, training data, and natural language processing
- See how automation will change jobs, including your own
- Identify the right projects and processes for applying AI tools
- Help your employees learn the essentials of AI
- Deal with ethical issues and biased results before they come up
- Select quality AI consultants and vendors and work with them effectively
- Build an AI team that fits your most pressing needs
- Communicate better with your machine learning experts and data scientists
- Make a plan for when algorithms make (inevitable) mistakes
- Scale AI across your organization

Contents

Introduction: How AI Will Redefine Management   1
Five practices that successful managers need to master.
BY VEGARD KOLBJØRNSRUD, RICHARD AMICO, AND ROBERT J. THOMAS

SECTION ONE
AI Fundamentals

1. Three Questions About AI That Every Employee Should Be Able to Answer   11
   How does it work, what is it good at, and what should it never do?
   BY EMMA MARTINHO-TRUSWELL

2. What Every Manager Should Know About Machine Learning   17
   A nontechnical primer.
   BY MIKE YEOMANS

3. The Three Types of AI   27
   First, understand which technologies perform which types of tasks.
   BY THOMAS H. DAVENPORT AND RAJEEV RONANKI

Contents

4. **AI Doesn't Have to Be Too Complicated or Expensive for Your Business** — 37
   Focus on data quality, not quantity.
   BY ANDREW NG

SECTION TWO
Building Your AI Team

5. **How AI Fits into Your Data Science Team** — 47
   Get over the cultural hurdles and avoid exaggerated claims.
   AN INTERVIEW WITH HILARY MASON
   BY WALTER FRICK

6. **Ramp Up Your Team's Predictive Analytics Skills** — 53
   Three pitfalls they need to avoid.
   BY ERIC SIEGEL

7. **Assembling Your AI Operations Team** — 61
   A top-notch model is no good if your people can't connect it to your existing systems.
   BY TERENCE TSE, MARK ESPOSITO, TAKAAKI MIZUNO, AND DANNY GOH

SECTION THREE
Picking the Right Projects

8. **How to Spot a Machine Learning Opportunity** — 71
   What do you want to predict, and do you have the data?
   BY KATHRYN HUME

9. **A Simple Tool to Start Making Decisions with the Help of AI**   79
   Use the AI Canvas.
   BY AJAY AGRAWAL, JOSHUA GANS, AND AVI GOLDFARB

10. **How to Pick the Right Automation Project**   89
    Invest in the ones that will build your organization's capabilities.
    BY BHASKAR GHOSH, RAJENDRA PRASAD, AND GAYATHRI PALLAIL

SECTION FOUR
Working with AI

11. **Collaborative Intelligence: Humans and AI Are Joining Forces**   97
    They're enhancing each other's strengths.
    BY H. JAMES WILSON AND PAUL DAUGHERTY

12. **How to Get Employees to Embrace AI**   117
    The sooner resisters get onboard, the sooner you will see results.
    BY BRAD POWER

13. **A Better Way to Onboard AI**   123
    Understand it as a tool to assist people rather than replace them.
    BY BORIS BABIC, DANIEL L. CHEN, THEODOROS EVGENIOU, AND ANNE-LAURE FAYARD

14. **Managing AI Decision-Making Tools**   139
    A framework to determine when and how humans need to stay involved.
    BY MICHAEL ROSS AND JAMES TAYLOR

Contents

15. **Your Company's Algorithms Will Go Wrong. Have a Plan in Place.** — 147

    An AI designed to do X will eventually fail to do X.

    BY ROMAN V. YAMPOLSKIY

SECTION FIVE

Managing Ethics and Bias

16. **A Practical Guide to Ethical AI** — 155

    AI doesn't just scale solutions—it also scales risk.

    BY REID BLACKMAN

17. **AI Can Help Address Inequity—If Companies Earn Users' Trust** — 167

    A case from Airbnb shows how good algorithms can have negative effects.

    BY SHUNYUAN ZHANG, KANNAN SRINIVASAN, PARAM VIR SINGH, AND NITIN MEHTA

18. **Take Action to Mitigate Ethical Risks** — 179

    It starts with three critical conversations.

    BY REID BLACKMAN AND BEENA AMMANATH

SECTION SIX

Taking the Next Steps with AI and Machine Learning

19. **How No-Code Platforms Can Bring AI to Small and Midsize Businesses** — 189

    Three features to look for as you consider the right tool for your company.

    BY JONATHON REILLY

20. **The Power of Natural Language Processing**   197

   NLP can help companies with brainstorming, summarizing, and researching.

   BY ROSS GRUETZEMACHER

21. **Reinforcement Learning Is Ready for Business**   205

   Learning through trial and error can lead to more creative solutions.

   BY KATHRYN HUME AND MATTHEW E. TAYLOR

EPILOGUE
Scaling AI

22. **How to Scale AI in Your Organization**   217

   Invest in processes, people, and tools.

   BY MANASI VARTAK

Appendix: Case Study: Will a Bank's New Technology Help or Hurt Morale?   225

   Weighing the benefits of AI against the downsides of impersonal decision-making.

   BY LEONARD A. SCHLESINGER

Glossary of Key AI Terms	*237*
Index	*243*

INTRODUCTION

How AI Will Redefine Management

by Vegard Kolbjørnsrud, Richard Amico, and Robert J. Thomas

Understanding AI and machine learning is no longer just the province of technology consultants, IT departments, and data scientists. Today, every leader and manager should know the practical basics of AI. Fortunately, it's possible for almost anyone to learn the fundamentals of how AI works and what kinds of tasks it does best.

Adapted from "How Artificial Intelligence Will Redefine Management," on hbr.org, November 2, 2016 (reprint #H0380Z).

Introduction

To find out how managers can thrive in the age of AI, we surveyed 1,770 managers from 14 countries and interviewed 37 executives in charge of digital transformation at their organizations. Using this data, we identified five practices that successful managers will need to master.

Leave Administration to AI

According to the survey, managers across all levels spend more than half of their time on administrative coordination and control tasks. (For instance, a typical store manager or a lead nurse at a nursing home must

FIGURE I-1

How managers spend their time

The bulk of it is spent on administrative tasks.

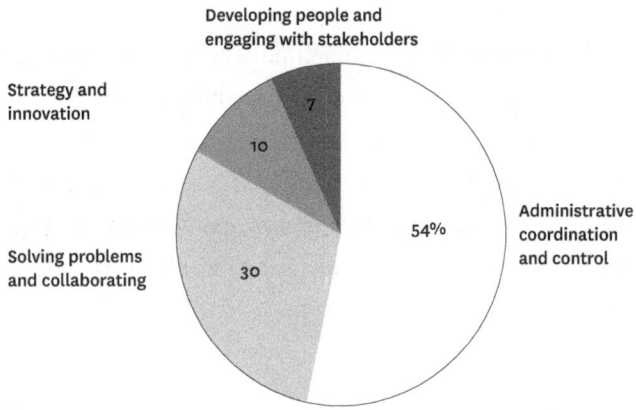

Percentage of time respondents spend on categories of work

Source: Accenture survey of 1,770 frontline, mid-level, and executive-level managers from 14 countries

constantly juggle shift schedules because of staff members' illnesses, vacations, or sudden departures.) These are the very responsibilities that the same managers expect to see AI affecting the most. And they are correct: AI will automate many of these tasks.

Report writing is another relevant example. The Associated Press expanded its quarterly earnings reporting from approximately 300 stories to 4,400 with the help of AI-powered software robots. In doing so, technology freed up journalists to conduct more investigative and interpretive reporting. Imagine technology like this drafting your next management report; in fact, this is already possible for some analytical management reports.

The managers we surveyed see such change in a positive light: Eighty-six percent said they would like AI support with monitoring and reporting.

Focus on Judgment Work

Many decisions require insight beyond what artificial intelligence can squeeze from data alone. Managers use their knowledge of organizational history and culture, as well as empathy and ethical reflection. This is the essence of human judgment—the application of experience and expertise to critical business decisions and practices. Managers we surveyed have a sense of a shift in this direction and identify the judgment-oriented skills of creative thinking and experimentation, data analysis and interpretation, and strategy development as three of the four top new skills that will be required to succeed in the future.

As Layne Thompson, director of ERP Services for a U.S. Navy IT organization, told us: "More often than not, managers think of what they're doing as requiring judgment, discretion, experience, and the capacity to improvise, as opposed to simply applying rules. And if one of the potential promises of machine learning is the ability to help make decisions, then we should think of technology as being intended to support rather than replace [managers]."

Treat Intelligent Machines as "Colleagues"

Managers who view AI as a kind of colleague will recognize that there's no need to "race against a machine." While human judgment is unlikely to be automated, intelligent machines can add enormously to this type of work, assisting in decision support and data-driven simulations as well as search and discovery activities. In fact, 78% of the surveyed managers believe that they will trust the advice of intelligent systems in making business decisions in the future.

One company that is trying to access these opportunities is the venture capital firm EQT Ventures, which uses its Motherbrain AI system to assess investment opportunities and identify unknown companies with big potential. The system scans a variety of sources and alerts EQT's investment professionals when it discovers an interesting startup. They in turn input their own leads and evaluations into the AI system, training it to better identify and assess leads. EQT strives to frame the software as a friendly and helpful colleague that provides relevant inputs and asks questions at the right time. At EQT, and many other firms, AI now serves managers as an always-available assistant and adviser.

Work Like a Designer

While managers' own creative abilities are vital, perhaps even more important is their ability to harness others' creativity. Manager-designers bring together diverse ideas into integrated, workable, and appealing solutions. They embed design thinking into the practices of their teams and organizations. A third of the managers in our survey identified creative thinking and experimentation as a key skill area they need to learn to stay successful as AI increasingly takes over administrative work.

In an interview, Peter Harmer, CEO of Insurance Australia Group, emphasized the need for managers who foster collaborative creativity in the digital enterprise: "We need people who can actually layer ideas on ideas. Not somebody who has to win in a competition around ideas, but somebody who can say, 'Crikey! If we bring these two or three or four things together, we've got something very, very different.' That's the creativity, the curiosity [we need in managers]."

Develop Social Skills and Networks

The managers we surveyed recognized the value of judgment work. But they undervalued the deep social skills critical to networking, coaching, and collaborating that will help them stand out in a world where AI carries out many of the administrative and analytical tasks they perform today.

Introduction

While these managers will use digital technologies to tap into the knowledge and judgment of partners, customers, and communities, they must be able to tease out and bring together diverse perspectives, insights, and experiences.

What This Book Will Do for You

AI will ultimately prove to be cheaper, more efficient, and potentially more impartial in its actions than human beings. But such a scenario should not be cause for concern for managers. It just means that their jobs will change to focus on things only humans can do.

Writing earnings reports is one thing but developing messages that can engage a workforce and provide a sense of purpose is human through and through. Tracking schedules and resources may soon fall within the jurisdiction of machines, but drafting strategy remains unmistakably human.

This book will help get you up to speed on topics such as building your AI team, picking the right projects, understanding AI ethics and bias, and scaling AI in your organization. If you're truly new to AI concepts, start with section 1 and read straight through. But if you already have a good grasp on the essentials, take a look at the table of contents and jump in at any chapter to deepen your knowledge. Be sure to take a look at the glossary at the end of this book for helpful definitions of key AI terms.

While oncoming disruptions won't arrive all at once, the pace of development is faster and the implications more far-reaching than most executives and managers realize. Just as technologies such as spreadsheets and visualization tools became must-use apps for managers, simple-to-use AI platforms that require little or no coding will soon be common. Those who are able to assess what the workforce of the future will look like can prepare themselves to thrive in the AI-enabled workplace. They should view it as an opportunity to flourish. Learning about the fundamentals of AI will set you on the right path.

Vegard Kolbjørnsrud is an associate professor at BI Norwegian Business School in Oslo, Norway, and a senior research fellow at Accenture. **Richard Amico** is a manager at Bain & Company, serving within the firm's macro trends group and global think tank, Bain Futures. **Robert J. Thomas** is a coach to top leadership teams. He is the author of eight books on leadership and organizational change, including *Crucibles of Leadership*, *Geeks and Geezers* (with Warren Bennis), and *Driving Results Through Social Networks* (with Robert L. Cross).

SECTION ONE
AI Fundamentals

CHAPTER 1

Three Questions About AI That Every Employee Should Be Able to Answer

by Emma Martinho-Truswell

Articles about artificial intelligence often begin with an intention to shock readers, referencing classic works of science fiction or alarming statistics about impending job losses. But I think we get closer to the heart of AI

Adapted from "Three Questions About AI That Nontechnical Employees Should Be Able to Answer," on hbr.org, August 2, 2018 (product #H04GEB).

today when we think about small and mundane ways in which AI makes work just a little easier. And it's not necessarily the AI experts in your organization who will identify these mundane problems that AI can help solve. Instead, employees throughout the organization will be able to spot the low-hanging fruit through which AI could make your organization more efficient. But only if they know what AI is capable of doing and what it should never do.

For example, I manage the finances for a team that travels very often, and I've been grateful for the intelligent guesswork that my expenses software extracts from receipts using machine learning: the merchant's name, the dollar amount spent, taxes, and likely expense categorization. Finding opportunities for this kind of clever improvement, saving human time and energy, is not just a leadership challenge. It's a search best undertaken by as many people within the organization as possible.

A fast-growing area of artificial intelligence is machine learning, in which a computer program improves its answers to a question by creating and iterating algorithms based on data. It is often regarded as the kind of technology that only the most clever and most mathematically minded people can understand and work with. Indeed, those who work day-to-day building machine learning programs will tend to have postgraduate degrees in computer science. But machine learning is a technological tool like any other: It can be understood on various levels and can still be used by those whose understanding is incomplete. People do not need to know how to fly a plane to be able to spot sensible new airline routes. Instead, they need to know approximately what a plane can and cannot do. For instance, lay people might also have ideas about what planes should *not* be used for, which could result in positive outcomes such as reducing aircraft noise in the middle of cities or limiting costly flights for very short journeys.

When leaders in companies, nonprofits, or governments invest in artificial intelligence, much of their attention goes to hiring machine learning experts or paying for tools. But this misses a critical opportunity. For organizations to get the most that they can from AI, they should also be investing in helping all of their team members to understand the technology better. Understanding machine learning can make an employee more likely to spot potential applications in their own work. Many of the most promising uses for machine learning will be humdrum, and this is where technology can be at its most useful: saving people time, so that they can concentrate on the many tasks at which they outperform machines. An executive assistant who has a better understanding of machine learning might suggest that calendar software learn more explicitly from patterns that develop over time, reminding them when their boss has not met with a team member for an unusually long time. A calendar that learns patterns could give an executive assistant more time for the human specialties of the job, such as helping their boss to manage a team.

So, what *should* all of your employees be learning about AI? Here are three important questions that any member of your team should be able to answer.

How does it work?

Team members who aren't responsible for building an AI system should nonetheless know how it processes information and answers questions. It's particularly important for people to understand the differences between how they learn and how a machine "learns." For example, a human trying to analyze 1 million data points will need to simplify the data in some way in order to make sense of it—perhaps by finding an average or creating a chart. A machine learning algorithm, on the other hand, can use every individual data point when it makes its calculations. They are "trained" to spot patterns using an existing set of data inputs and outputs. Because data is fundamental to a machine's ability to provide useful answers, a manager should ensure that their team members have some basic data literacy. This means helping people to understand what numbers are telling us and what biases and errors might be hidden within them. Understanding data—the fuel of AI—helps people to understand what AI is good at.

What is it good at?

Machine learning tools excel when they can be trained to solve a problem using vast quantities of reliable data and to give answers within clear parameters that people have defined for them. My expenses software is a perfect example: It has the receipts of its millions of users to learn from, and it uses them to help predict whether a cup of coffee from Starbucks should be categorized as travel, stationery, or entertainment. Learning what machine learning is good at quickly helps someone to see what machine learning is *not* good at. Problems that are novel, or which lack meaningful data to explain them, remain squarely in the realm of human specialties. Help your employees to understand this difference by showing them tools they already use that are powered by AI either within the organization or outside it (such as social media advertising or streaming service recommendations). These examples will help team members to understand AI's enormous potential and also its limitations.

What should it never do?

Just because machine learning can solve a problem does not mean it should do so. A machine cannot understand the biases that data reveals, for example, nor the consequences of the advice it gives. There may be some problems that your organization should never ask an AI application to solve. For example, I would not want an algorithm to make the final decision for my company on whom to hire, what to discuss at a board meeting, or how to manage a poorly performing staff member. If employees have thought about proper ethical limitations of AI, they can be important guards against its misuse.

The organizations that will do best in the age of artificial intelligence will be good at finding opportunities for AI to help employees do their day-to-day jobs better and will be able to implement those ideas quickly. They will be clear about where to deploy machine learning and where to avoid it. Alongside their investments in technology, they will remind their teams of the importance of human specialties: supporting colleagues, communicating well, and experimenting with novel ideas. To be ready for pervasive AI, an organization's whole team will need to be ready too.

Emma Martinho-Truswell is the cofounder and COO of Oxford Insights, which advises organizations on the strategic, cultural, and leadership opportunities from digital transformation and artificial intelligence.

CHAPTER 2

What Every Manager Should Know About Machine Learning

by Mike Yeomans

It seems as though every week companies are finding new uses for algorithms that adapt as they encounter new data. As managers navigate these advances, it is helpful to think of machine learning simply as a branch of statistics, designed for a world of big data. Those who want to get the most out of their companies' data should

---

Adapted from content posted on hbr.org, July 7, 2015 (product #H026NG).

understand what it is, what it can do, and what to watch out for when using it.

Not Just Big Data but Wide Data

The enormous scale of data available to firms can pose several challenges. Of course, big data may require advanced software and hardware to handle and store it. But machine learning is about how the analysis of the data also has to adapt to the size of the data set. This is because big data is not just *long*, but *wide* as well. Consider an online retailer's database of customers in a spreadsheet. Each customer gets a row, and if there are lots of customers then the data set will be *long*. However, every variable in the data gets its own column, too, and we can now collect so much data on every customer—purchase history, browser history, mouse clicks, text from reviews—that the data is usually *wide* as well, to the point where there are even more columns than rows. Most of the tools in machine learning are designed to make better use of wide data.

Predictions, Not Causality

The most common application of machine learning tools is to make predictions. Here are a few examples of prediction problems in a business:

- Making personalized recommendations for customers

- Forecasting long-term customer loyalty

- Anticipating the future performance of employees
- Rating the credit risk of loan applicants

These settings share some common features. For one, they are all complex environments, where the right decision might depend on a lot of variables (which means they require "wide" data). They also have some outcome to validate the results of a prediction—like whether someone clicks on a recommended item or whether a customer buys again. Finally, there is an important business decision to be made that requires an accurate prediction.

One important difference from traditional statistics is that you're not focused on *causality* in machine learning. That is, you might not need to know what happens when you change the environment. Instead you are focusing on *prediction*, which means you might only need a model of the environment to make the right decision. This is just like deciding whether to leave the house with an umbrella: We have to predict the weather before we decide whether to bring one. The weather forecast is very helpful, but it is limited; the forecast might not tell you how clouds work or how the umbrella works, and it won't tell you how to change the weather. The same goes for machine learning: Personalized recommendations are forecasts of people's preferences, and they are helpful, even if they won't tell you why people like the things they do or how to change what they like. If you keep these limitations in mind, the value of machine learning will be a lot more obvious.

TABLE 2-1

What machine learning can do

A simple way to think about supervised learning.

Input A	Response B	Application
Picture	Are there human faces? (0 or 1)	Photo tagging
Loan application	Will they repay the loan? (0 or 1)	Loan approvals
Ad plus user information	Will user click on ad? (0 or 1)	Targeted online ads
Audio clip	Transcript of audio clip	Speech recognition
English sentence	French sentence	Language translation
Sensors from hard disk, plane engine, etc.	Is it about to fail?	Preventive maintenance
Car camera and other sensors	Position of other cars	Self-driving cars

Source: Andrew Ng, "What Artificial Intelligence Can and Can't Do Right Now," hbr.org, November 9, 2016, https://hbr.org/2016/11/what-artificial-intelligence-can-and-cant-do-right-now.

Separating the Signal from the Noise

So far we've talked about when machine learning can be useful. But how is it used, in practice? It would be impossible to cover it all in one article, but roughly speaking there are three broad concepts that capture most of what goes on under the hood of a machine learning algorithm: *feature extraction*, which determines what data to use in the model; *regularization*, which determines how the data is weighted within the model; and *cross-validation*, which tests the accuracy of the model. Each of these factors helps us identify and separate "signal" (valuable, consistent relationships that we want to learn) from "noise" (random correlations that won't occur again in the future, which we want to avoid). Every data set has a mix of signal and noise, and these concepts will help you sort through that mix to make better predictions.

Feature Extraction

Think of feature extraction as the process of figuring out what variables the model will use. Sometimes this can simply mean dumping all the raw data straight in, but many machine learning techniques can build new variables—called "features"—which can aggregate important signals that are spread out over many variables in the raw data. In this case the signal would be too diluted to have an effect without feature extraction. One example of feature extraction is in face recognition, where the features are actual facial features—nose length, eye color, skin tone, etc.—that are calculated with information from many different pixels in an image. In a music store, you could have features for different genres. For instance, you could combine all the rock sales into a single feature, all the classical sales into another feature, and so on.

There are many different ways to extract features, and the most useful ones are often automated. That means that rather than handpicking the genre for each album, you can find clusters of albums that tend to be bought by all the same people and learn the genres from the data (and you might even discover new genres you didn't know existed). This is also very common with text data, where you can extract underlying topics of discussion based on which words and phrases tend to appear together in the same documents. However, domain experts can still be helpful in suggesting features and in making sense of the clusters that the machine finds.

(Clustering is a complex problem, and sometimes these tools are used just to organize data, rather than make a prediction. This type of machine learning is called "unsupervised learning," because there is no measured outcome that is being used as a target for prediction.)

Regularization

How do you know if the features you've extracted actually reflect signal rather than noise? Intuitively, you want to tell your model to play it safe, not to jump to any conclusions. This idea is called "regularization." (The same idea is reflected in terms like "pruning," "shrinkage," or "variable selection.") To illustrate, imagine the most conservative model possible: It would make the same prediction for everyone. In a music store, for example, this means recommending the most popular album to every person, no matter what else they liked. This approach deliberately ignores both signal and noise. At the other end of the spectrum, we could build a complex, flexible model that tries to accommodate every little quirk in a customer's data. This model would learn from both signal and noise. The problem is, if there's too much noise in your data, the flexible model could be even worse than the conservative baseline. This is called "overfitting": The model is learning patterns that won't hold up in future cases.

Regularization is a way to split the difference between a flexible model and a conservative model, and this is usually calculated by adding a penalty for complexity, which forces the model to stay simple. There are two kinds of effects that this penalty can have on a model. One effect, selection, is when the algorithm focuses on only a few features that contain the best signal and discards the others. Another effect, shrinkage, is when the algorithm reduces each feature's influence, so that the predictions aren't overly reliant on any one feature in case it turns out to be noisy.

Cross-Validation

Once you have built a model, how can you be sure it is making good predictions? The most important test is whether the model is accurate "out of sample," which is when the model is making predictions for data it has never seen before. This is important because eventually you will want to use the model to make new decisions, and you need to know it can do that reliably. However, it can be costly to run tests in the field, and you can be a lot more efficient by using the data you already have to simulate an out-of-sample test of prediction accuracy. This is most commonly done in machine learning with a process called cross-validation.

Imagine we are building a prediction model using data on 10,000 past customers and we want to know how accurate the predictions will be for future customers. A simple way to estimate that accuracy is to randomly split the sample into two parts: a training set of 9,000 to build the model and a test set of 1,000, which is initially put aside. Once we've finished building a model with the training set, we can see how well the model predicts the outcomes in the test set, as a dry run. The most important thing is that the model never sees the test set outcomes until after it is built. If you don't keep a clear partition between these two, you will overestimate how good your model actually is, which can be a very costly mistake to make.

Mistakes to Avoid When Using Machine Learning

One of the easiest traps in machine learning is to confuse a prediction model with a causal model. Humans are hardwired to think about how to change the environment to cause an effect. In prediction problems, however, causality isn't a priority: Instead we're trying to optimize a decision that depends on a stable environment. In fact, the more stable an environment, the more useful a prediction model will be.

It's important to draw a distinction between "out of sample" and "out of context." Measuring out-of-sample accuracy means that if we collect new data from the exact same environment, the model will be able to predict the outcomes well. However, there is no guarantee the model will be as useful if we move to a new environment. For example, an online store might use a database of online purchases to build a helpful model for new customers. But the exact same model may not be helpful for customers in a brick-and-mortar store—even if the product line is identical.

It's tempting to think that the sheer size of data available can get around the issue. That's not the case. Remember, these algorithms draw their power from being able to compare new cases to a large database of similar cases from the past. When you try to apply a model in a different context, the cases in the database may not be so similar anymore, and what was a strength in the original context is now a liability. There's no easy answer to this problem. An out-of-context model can still be an improvement over no model at all, as long as its limitations are taken into consideration.

Even though some parts of model-building can seem automatic, it still takes a healthy dose of human judgment to figure out where a model will be useful. Furthermore, there's a lot of critical thinking that goes into making sure the built-in safeguards of regularization and cross-validation are being used the right way.

But it's also good to keep in mind that the alternative—purely human judgment—comes with its own set of biases and errors. With the right mix of technical skill and human judgment, machine learning can be a useful new tool for decision-makers trying to make sense of the inherent problems of wide data. Hopefully without creating new problems along the way.

Mike Yeomans is an assistant professor at Imperial College Business School.

CHAPTER 3

The Three Types of AI

by Thomas H. Davenport and Rajeev Ronanki

It is useful for companies to look at AI through the lens of business capabilities rather than technologies. Broadly speaking, AI can support three important business needs: automating business processes, gaining insight through data analysis, and engaging with customers and employees. This article is based on a study we conducted that reviewed 152 AI projects across many organizations. Let's look at the three types in turn.

1. Process Automation

Robotic process automation (RPA) technologies automate digital and physical tasks—typically back-office

---

Adapted from "Artificial Intelligence for the Real World" in *Harvard Business Review*, January–February 2018 (product #R1801H).

administrative and financial activities. RPA is more advanced than earlier business-process automation tools, because the "robots" (that is, code on a server) act like a human inputting and consuming information from multiple IT systems. Tasks include:

- Transferring data from email and call center systems into systems of record—for example, updating customer files with address changes or service additions

- Replacing lost credit or ATM cards, reaching into multiple systems to update records and handle customer communications

- Reconciling failures to charge for services across billing systems by extracting information from multiple document types

- "Reading" legal and contractual documents to extract provisions using natural language processing

RPA is the least expensive and easiest to implement of the cognitive technologies we'll discuss here and typically brings a quick and high return on investment. (It's also the least "smart" in the sense that these applications aren't programmed to learn and improve, though developers are slowly adding more intelligence and learning capability.) It is particularly well suited to working across multiple back-end systems.

At NASA, cost pressures led the agency to launch four RPA pilots in accounts payable and receivable, IT spending, and human resources—all managed by a shared services center. The four projects worked well—in the HR application, for example, 86% of transactions were completed without human intervention—and are being rolled out across the organization. NASA continued to implement more RPA bots, some with higher levels of intelligence.

One might imagine that robotic process automation would quickly put people out of work. But across the 71 RPA projects we reviewed, replacing administrative employees was neither the primary objective nor a common outcome. Only a few projects led to reductions in head count, and in most cases, the tasks in question had already been shifted to outsourced workers. As technology improves, robotic automation projects are likely to lead to some job losses in the future, particularly in the offshore business-process outsourcing industry. If you can outsource a task, you can probably automate it.

2. Cognitive Insight

These projects use algorithms to detect patterns in vast volumes of data and interpret their meaning. Think of it as "analytics on steroids." These machine learning applications are being used to:

- Predict what a particular customer is likely to buy

- Identify credit fraud in real time and detect insurance claims fraud

- Analyze warranty data to identify safety or quality problems in automobiles and other manufactured products

- Automate personalized targeting of digital ads
- Provide insurers with more accurate and detailed actuarial modeling

Cognitive insights provided by machine learning differ from those available from traditional analytics in three ways: They are usually much more data-intensive and detailed, the models typically are trained on some part of the data set, and the models get better—that is, their ability to use new data to make predictions or put things into categories improves over time.

Versions of machine learning (deep learning, in particular, which attempts to mimic the activity in the human brain in order to recognize patterns) can perform feats such as recognizing images and speech. Machine learning can also make available new data for better analytics. While the activity of data curation has historically been quite labor-intensive, now machine learning can identify probabilistic matches—data that is likely to be associated with the same person or company but that appears in slightly different formats—across databases. A large bank used this technology to extract data on terms from supplier contracts and match it with invoice numbers, identifying tens of millions of dollars in products and services not supplied. Deloitte's audit practice is using cognitive insight to extract terms from contracts, which enables an audit to address a much higher proportion of documents, often 100%, without human auditors' having to painstakingly read through them.

Cognitive insight applications are typically used to improve performance on jobs only machines can do—

tasks such as programmatic ad buying that involve such high-speed data crunching and automation that they've long been beyond human ability—so they're not generally a threat to human jobs.

3. Cognitive Engagement

Projects that engage employees and customers using natural language processing chatbots, intelligent agents, and machine learning were the least common type in our study. This category includes:

- Intelligent agents that offer 24/7 customer service addressing a broad and growing array of issues from password requests to technical support questions—all in the customer's natural language

- Internal sites for answering employee questions on topics including IT, employee benefits, and HR policy

- Product and service recommendation systems for retailers that increase personalization, engagement, and sales—typically including rich language or images

- Health treatment recommendation systems that help providers create customized care plans that take into account individual patients' health status and previous treatments

The companies in our study tended to use cognitive engagement technologies more to interact with employees than with customers. That may change as firms become more comfortable turning customer interactions over to machines. Vanguard, for example, is piloting an intelligent agent that helps its customer service staff answer frequently asked questions. The plan is to eventually allow customers to engage with the cognitive agent directly, rather than with the human customer-service agents. SEB, a bank in Sweden, and the medical technology giant Becton, Dickinson, in the United States, are using the lifelike intelligent-agent avatar Amelia to serve as an internal employee help desk for IT support. SEB made Amelia available to customers on a limited basis in order to test its performance and customer response.

In most of the projects we studied, the goal was not to reduce head count but to handle growing numbers of employee and customer interactions without adding staff. Some organizations were planning to hand over routine communications to machines, while transitioning customer-support personnel to more-complex activities such as handling customer issues that escalate, conducting extended unstructured dialogues, or reaching out to customers before they call in with problems.

As companies become more familiar with cognitive tools, they are experimenting with projects that combine elements from all three categories to reap the benefits of AI. An Italian insurer, for example, developed a "cognitive help desk" within its IT organization. The system engages with employees using deep-learning technology (part of the cognitive insights category) to search frequently asked questions and answers, previously resolved cases, and documentation to come up with solutions to employees' problems. It employs a smart-routing capability (business process automation) to forward the most complex problems to human representatives, and it uses natural language processing to support user requests in Italian.

Understanding the Technologies

Before embarking on an AI initiative, companies must understand which technologies perform what types of tasks, and the strengths and limitations of each. Rule-based expert systems and robotic process automation, for example, are transparent in how they do their work, but neither is capable of learning nor improving. Deep learning, on the other hand, is great at learning from large volumes of labeled data, but it's almost impossible to understand how it creates the models it does. This "black-box" issue can be problematic in highly regulated industries such as financial services, in which regulators insist on knowing why decisions are made in a certain way.

We encountered several organizations that wasted time and money pursuing the wrong technology for the job at hand. If they're armed with a good understanding of the different technologies, companies are better positioned to determine which might best address specific needs, which vendors to work with, and how quickly a system can be implemented. Acquiring this understanding requires ongoing research and education, usually within IT or an innovation group.

In particular, companies will need to leverage the capabilities of key employees, such as data scientists, who have the statistical and big-data skills necessary to learn the nuts and bolts of these technologies. A main success factor is your people's willingness to learn. Some will leap at the opportunity, while others will want to stick with tools they're familiar with. Strive to have a high percentage of the former.

If you don't have data science or analytics capabilities in-house, you'll probably have to build an ecosystem of external service providers in the near term. If you expect to be implementing longer-term AI projects, you will want to recruit expert in-house talent. Either way, having the right capabilities is essential to progress.

Given the scarcity of cognitive technology talent, most organizations should establish a pool of resources—perhaps in a centralized function such as IT or strategy—and make experts available to high-priority projects throughout the organization. As needs and talent proliferate, it may make sense to dedicate groups to particular business functions or units, but even then, a central coordinating function can be useful in managing projects and careers.

We believe that every large company should be exploring cognitive technologies. There will be some bumps in the road, and there is no room for complacency on issues of workforce displacement and the ethics of smart machines. But with the right planning and development, cognitive technology could usher in a golden age of productivity, work satisfaction, and prosperity.

Thomas H. Davenport is the President's Distinguished Professor of Information Technology and Management at Babson College, a visiting professor at Oxford's Saïd School of Business, a research fellow at the MIT Initiative on the Digital Economy, and a senior adviser to Deloitte's AI practice. **Rajeev Ronanki** is a senior vice president at Elevance Health. He was previously a principal at Deloitte Consulting, where he led the cognitive computing and health care innovation practices. Some of the companies mentioned in this article are Deloitte clients.

CHAPTER 4

AI Doesn't Have to Be Too Complicated or Expensive for Your Business

by Andrew Ng

Despite the vast potential of AI, it hasn't caught hold in most industries. Sure, it has transformed consumer internet companies such as Google, Baidu, and Amazon—all massive and data rich, with hundreds of millions of users. But industries such as manufacturing, agriculture,

---

Adapted from content posted on hbr.org, July 29, 2021 (product #H06HSP).

and health care still need to find ways to make this technology work for them. Here's the problem: The playbook that these consumer internet companies use to build their AI systems—where a single one-size-fits-all AI system can serve massive numbers of users—won't perform well for these other industries.

Instead, these legacy industries will need a large number of bespoke solutions that are adapted to their many diverse use cases. This doesn't mean that AI won't work for them, however. It just means they need to take a different approach.

To bridge this gap and unleash AI's full potential, executives in all industries should adopt a new, data-centric approach to building AI. They should aim to build AI systems with careful attention to ensuring that the data clearly conveys what they need the AI to learn. This requires focusing on data that covers important cases and is consistently labeled, so that the AI can learn from this data what it is supposed to do. In other words, the key to creating these valuable AI systems is programming with data rather than with code.

Why Adopting AI Outside of Tech Can Be So Hard

Why isn't AI widely used outside consumer internet companies? The top challenges facing AI adoption in other industries include:

1. **Small data sets.** In a consumer internet company with huge numbers of users, engineers have millions of data points that their AI can learn

from. But in other industries, the data set sizes are much smaller. For example, can you build an AI system that learns to detect a defective automotive component after seeing only 50 examples? Or to detect a rare disease after learning from just 100 diagnoses? Techniques built for 50 million data points don't work when you have only 50 data points.

2. **Cost of customization.** Consumer internet companies employ dozens or hundreds of skilled engineers to build and maintain monolithic AI systems that create tremendous value—say, an online ad system that generates more than $1 billion in revenue per year. But in other industries, there are numerous $1 million–$5 million projects, each of which needs a custom AI system. For example, each factory manufacturing a different type of product might require a custom inspection system, and every hospital, with its own way of coding health records, might need its own AI to process its patient data. The aggregate value of these hundreds of thousands of projects is massive, but the economics of an individual project might not support hiring a large, dedicated AI team to build and maintain it. This problem is exacerbated by the ongoing shortage of AI talent.

3. **Gap between proof of concept and production.** Even when an AI system works in the lab, a massive amount of engineering is needed to deploy it in production. It is not unusual for teams to

celebrate a successful proof of concept, only to realize that they still have another 12–24 months of work before the system can be deployed and maintained.

For AI to realize its full potential, we need a systematic approach to solving these problems across all industries. The data-centric approach to AI, supported by tools designed for building, deploying, and maintaining AI applications—called machine learning operations (MLOps) platforms—will make this possible.

Data-Centric AI Development

AI systems are made up of software—the computer program that includes an AI model—and data, the information used to train the model. For example, to build an AI system for automated inspection in manufacturing, an AI engineer might create software that implements a deep learning algorithm, which is then shown a data set comprising pictures of good and defective parts so it can learn to distinguish between them.

Over the last decade, a lot of AI research was driven by software-centric development (also called *model-centric development*) in which the data is fixed and teams attempt to optimize or invent new programs to learn from the available data. Many tech companies had large data sets from millions of consumers, and they used these to drive a lot of innovation in AI.

But at AI's current level of sophistication, the bottleneck for many applications is getting the right data to feed to the software. We've heard about the benefits of *big data*, but we now know that for many applications, it is more fruitful to focus on making sure we have *good data*—data that clearly illustrates the concepts we need the AI to learn. This means, for example, the data should be reasonably comprehensive in its coverage of important cases and labeled consistently. Data is food for AI, and modern AI systems need not only calories but also high-quality nutrition.

Shifting your focus from software to data offers an important advantage: It relies on the people you already have on staff. In a time of great AI talent shortage, a data-centric approach allows many subject matter experts who have vast knowledge of their respective industries to contribute to the AI system development.

For example, most factories have workers who are highly skilled at defining and identifying what counts as a defect (is a 0.2 mm scratch a defect or is it so small that it doesn't matter?). If we expect each factory to ask its workers to invent new AI software as a way to get that factory the bespoke solution it needs, progress will be slow. But if we instead build and provide tools to empower these domain experts to engineer the data—by allowing them to express their knowledge about manufacturing through providing data to the AI—their odds of success will be much higher.

Make Building and Using AI Systematic and Repeatable

The shift toward data-centric AI development is being enabled by the emerging field of MLOps, which provide tools that make building, deploying, and maintaining AI systems easier than ever before. Tools that are geared to help produce high-quality data sets, in particular, hold the key to addressing the challenges of small data sets, high cost of customization, and the long road to getting an AI project into production outlined above.

How, exactly? First, ensuring high-quality data means that AI systems will be able to learn from the smaller data sets available in most industries. Second, by making it possible for a business's domain experts, rather than AI experts, to engineer the data, the ability to use AI will become more accessible to all industries. And third, MLOps platforms provide much of the scaffolding software needed to take an AI system to production, so teams no longer have to develop this software. This allows teams to deploy AI systems—and bridge the gap between proof of concept and production in weeks or months rather than years.

The vast majority of valuable AI projects have yet to be imagined. And even for projects that teams are already working on, the gap that leads to deployment in production remains to be bridged—indeed, Accenture estimates that 80% to 85% of companies' AI projects are in the proof-of-concept stage.

Here are some things companies can do right now:

1. Instead of merely focusing on the *quantity* of data you collect, also consider the *quality*; make sure it clearly illustrates the concepts you need the AI to learn.

2. Make sure your team considers taking a data-centric approach rather than a software-centric

approach. Many AI engineers, including many with strong academic or research backgrounds, were trained to take a software-centric approach; urge them to adopt data-centric techniques as well.

3. For any AI project that you intend to take to production, be sure to plan the deployment process and provide MLOps tools to support it. For example, even while building a proof-of-concept system, urge the teams to begin developing a longer-term plan for data management, deployment, and AI system monitoring and maintenance.

It's possible for AI to become a thriving asset outside of data-rich consumer internet businesses, but it has yet to hit its stride in other industries. A new data-centric mindset, coupled with MLOps tools that allow industry domain experts to participate in the creation, deployment, and maintenance of AI systems, will ensure that all industries can reap the rewards that AI can offer.

Andrew Ng is the founder and CEO of Landing AI, the former VP and chief scientist of Baidu, cochairman and cofounder of Coursera, the former founding lead of Google Brain, and an adjunct professor at Stanford University.

SECTION TWO

Building Your AI Team

CHAPTER 5

How AI Fits into Your Data Science Team

An interview with Hilary Mason by Walter Frick

How should we put AI into practice? Where in the organization should these capabilities sit, and how should companies take advantage of them? To get a practical, on-the-ground view, HBR senior editor Walter Frick spoke with Hilary Mason, the founder of Fast Forward Labs, a machine intelligence research firm. Here are excerpts from their conversation.

HBR: As a data scientist and a researcher, how do you think about the recent progress in your field?

Adapted from content posted on hbr.org, July 21, 2017 (product #H03QYC).

Mason: If we were having this conversation in the late 2000s, it would have been about big data—about whether we could even build the infrastructure to get all the data into one place and to query it. Once you can do that, you can do analytics, which is essentially counting things to answer questions that have business value or product value. People could always count things in data, but the change we saw about around 2009 was that new software made doing it affordable and accessible for a wide variety of people who never could do it before.

And that led to the rise of data science, which is about counting things cleverly, predicting things, and building models on data. Because that modeling was now so much cheaper, it was applied not just to very high-value problems, like actuarial science, but to things that may seem fairly trivial, like recommendations, search results, and that kind of stuff.

Then we had machine learning, which is a set of tools inside data science that let you count things cleverly and incorporate feedback loops. We began using the models to get more data from the world, and then fed the data back into those models so that they improved over time.

Now, today, we talk about AI. The term itself is a little bit loose—it has both a technical meaning and a marketing meaning—but it's essentially about using machine learning, and specifically deep learning, to enable applications that are built on top of this stack. That means that you can't do AI without machine learning. You also can't do machine learning without analytics, and you can't do analytics without data infrastructure. And so that's how I see them all being related.

How do machine learning and AI fit into companies' existing data capabilities?

Data science is used in multiple ways inside an organization, and a really common mistake I see people make in managing it is assuming that because it runs on one tech stack, it's just one thing. But I'd break it down into three capabilities, all of which rely on the same technology. The first capability is understanding the business. That's analytics, or business intelligence—being able to ask questions and analyze information to make better decisions. It's usually run out of the CFO or COO's office. It's not necessarily a technical domain.

The second capability is product data science: building algorithms and systems—which may use machine learning and AI—that actually improve the product. This is where things like spam filters, recommendation systems, search algorithms, and data visualization come in. This capability usually sits under a line of business and is run out of product development or engineering.

The last data capability is one that tends to get neglected or lumped in with product data science. It's an R&D capability—using data to open up new product, new business, and new revenue opportunities.

Are all three capabilities changed by machine learning and AI?

Let's look more closely at what deep learning offers, since it's central to a lot of what people now call AI and is a big part of the progress in machine learning in recent years. First, deep learning makes data accessible that was previously inaccessible to any kind of analysis—you can actually find value in video and audio data, for example. The number of companies that have a large amount of that kind of data is still fairly small, but I do think it's likely to increase over time. Even analytics is impacted by the ability to use image data rather than just text or structured data. Second, deep learning enables new approaches to solving very difficult data science problems—text summarization, for example. Deep learning allows you to create predictive models at a level of quality and sophistication that was previously out of reach. And so deep learning also enhances the product function of data science because it can generate new product opportunities. For example, several companies are using deep learning very successfully in e-commerce recommendation systems. Then, of course, deep learning affects the R&D function by pushing the frontier of what is technically possible.

What other mistakes do you see companies making in their data science efforts?

A big one involves process. We've noticed that people shoehorn this kind of stuff into the software engineering process, and that doesn't work. Developing data science systems is fundamentally different in several ways. At the outset of a data science project, you don't know if it's going to work. At the outset of a software engineering project, you know it's going to work.

This means that software engineering processes fail when they encounter uncertainty. By contrast, data science requires an experimental process that allows for uncertainty.

Also, every company has its own cultural hurdle to get over. A lot of companies aren't places where you can work on something that doesn't succeed, so the poor data scientists who do the risky research projects end up getting penalized in their annual reviews because they worked on something for two months that didn't pay off, even though they did great work. Data science requires having that cultural space to experiment and work on things that might fail. Companies need to understand that they're investing in a portfolio of initiatives, some of which will eventually pay off, generating dramatically more value than incremental product improvements do.

How do you navigate all the buzz around this topic, and how do you recommend executives do so?

I remain a relentless optimist about the potential of what we're now calling AI, but I'm also a pragmatist in the sense that I need to deliver systems that work to our clients, and that is quite a constraint. There are some folks running around making claims that are clearly exaggerated and ridiculous. In other cases, things that a few years ago we would have called regression analysis are now being called AI, just to enhance their value from a marketing perspective. So my advice is to keep in mind that there is no magic. At a conceptual level nothing here is out of reach of any executive's understanding. And if someone is pitching you on an idea and says, "I don't want to explain how it works, but it's AI," it's really important to keep asking: How does it work? What data goes in? What patterns might be in the data that the system could be learning? And what comes out? Because what comes out of a deep learning system is generally just a previously unlabeled data point that now has a label, along with some confidence in that label, and that's it. It's not intelligent in the sense that you and I are—and we're still a long, long way away from anything that looks like the kind of intelligence that a human has.

Hilary Mason is the GM for machine learning at Cloudera. She was the founder of Fast Forward Labs, acquired by Cloudera, in 2017 and is the data scientist in residence at Accel.

CHAPTER 6

Ramp Up Your Team's Predictive Analytics Skills

by Eric Siegel

With today's high demand for data scientists and the high salaries that they command, it's often not practical for companies to keep them on staff. Instead, many organizations work to ramp up their existing staff's analytics skills, including predictive analytics. But organizations need to proceed with caution. Predictive analytics is especially easy to get wrong. Here are the first three

---

Adapted from "3 Common Mistakes That Can Derail Your Team's Predictive Analytics Efforts," on hbr.org, October 5, 2018 (product #H04KHM).

"don'ts" your team needs to learn, and their corresponding remedies.

Don't Fall for Buzzwords. Clarify Your Objective.

As fashionable as it is, "data science" is not a business objective or a learning objective in and of itself. This buzzword means nothing more specific than "some clever use of data." It doesn't necessarily refer to any particular technology, method, or value proposition. Rather, it alludes to a culture—one of smart people doing creative things to find value in their data. It's important for everyone to keep this top of mind when learning to work with data.

Under the wide umbrella of data science sits predictive analytics, which delivers the most actionable win you can get from data. In a nutshell, predictive analytics is technology that learns from experience (data) to predict the future behavior of individuals in order to drive better decisions. Prediction is the holy grail for more effectively executing mass scale operations in marketing, financial risk, fraud detection, and beyond. Predictive analytics empowers your organization to optimize these functions by flagging who's most likely to click, buy, lie, die, commit fraud, quit their job, or cancel their subscription—and, beyond predicting people, by also foretelling the most likely outcomes for individual corporate clients and financial instruments. These predictions directly inform the action to take with each individual, e.g., by marketing to those most likely to buy and auditing those most likely to commit fraud.

In their application to these business functions, *predictive analytics* and *machine learning (ML)* are synonyms (in other arenas, machine learning also extends to tasks such as facial recognition that aren't usually called predictive analytics). Machine learning is key to prediction. The accumulation of patterns or formulas ML derives (learns) from the data—known as a *predictive model*—serves to consider a unique situation and put odds on the outcome. For example, the model could take as input everything currently known about an individual customer and produce as output the probability that that individual will cancel their subscription.

When you begin to deploy predictive analytics with your team, you're embarking upon a new kind of value proposition, and so it requires a new kind of leadership process. You'll need some team members to become "machine learning leaders" or "predictive analytics managers"—which signify much more specific skill sets than the catch-all "data scientist," a title that's guilty of vagaries and overhype (but do allow them that title if they like, as long as you're on the same page).

Don't Lead with Software Selection. Team Skills Come First.

In 2011, Thomas Davenport was kind enough to keynote at the conference I founded, Predictive Analytics World. "It's not about the math—it's about the people!" he absolutely bellowed at our captivated audience, more loudly than I'd heard since high school, when teachers had to get control of a classroom of teens.

Tom's startling tone struck just the right note (a high D flat, to be exact). Analytics vendors will tell you their software is The Solution. But the solution to what? The problem at hand is to optimize your large-scale operations. And the solution is a new way of business that integrates machine learning. So, a machine learning tool only serves a small part of what must be a holistic organizational process.

Rather than following a vendor's lead, prepare your staff to manage machine learning integration as an enterprise endeavor, and then allow your staff to determine a more informed choice of analytics software during a later stage of the project.

Don't Leap to the Number Crunching. Strategically Plan the Deployment.

The most common mistake that derails predictive analytics projects is jumping into machine learning before establishing a path to operational deployment. Predictive analytics isn't a technology you simply buy and plug in. It's an organizational paradigm that must bridge the quant/business culture gap by way of a collaborative process guided jointly by strategic, operational, and analytical stakeholders.

Each predictive analytics project follows a relatively standard, established series of steps that begins first with establishing how it will be deployed by your business and then works backward to see what you need to predict and what data you need to predict it, as follows:

1. **Establish the business objective**—how the predictive model will be integrated in order to actively

make a positive impact on existing operations, such as by more effectively targeting customer retention marketing campaigns.

2. **Define a specific prediction objective** to serve the business objective, for which you must have buy-in from business stakeholders—such as marketing staff, who must be willing to change their targeting accordingly. Here's an example: *"Which current customers with a tenure of at least one year and who have purchased more than $500 to date will cancel within three months and not rejoin for another three months thereafter?"* In practice, business tactics and pragmatic constraints will often mean the prediction objective must be even more specifically defined than that.

3. **Prepare the training data** that machine learning will operate on. This can be a significant bottleneck, generally expected to require 80% of the project's hands-on workload. It's a database-programming task, by which your existing data in its current form is rejiggered for the needs of machine learning software.

4. **Apply machine learning** to generate the predictive model. This is the "rocket science" part, but it isn't the most time-intensive. It's the stage where the choice of analytics tool counts—but, initially, software options may be tried out and compared with free evaluation licenses before a decision is made about which one to buy (or which free open source tool to use).

5. **Deploy the model.** Integrate its predictions into existing operations. For example, target a retention campaign to the top 5% of customers for whom an affirmative answer to the "will the customer cancel" question defined in step 2 is most probable.

There are two things you should know about these steps before selecting training options for your predictive analytics leaders. First, these five steps involve extensive backtracking and iteration. For example, only by executing step 3 might it become clear there isn't sufficient data for the prediction objective established in step 2, in which case it must be revisited and modified.

Second, at least for your first pilot projects, you'll need to bring in an external machine learning consultant for key parts of the process. Normally, your staff shouldn't endeavor to immediately become autonomous hands-on practitioners of the core machine learning, i.e., step 4. While it's important for project leaders to learn the fundamental principles behind how the technology works—in order to understand both its data requirements and the meaning of the predictive probabilities it outputs—a quantitative expert with prior predictive analytics projects in their portfolio should step in for step 4, and also help guide steps 2 and 3. This can be a relatively light engagement that keeps the overall project cost-effective, since you'll still internally execute the most time-intensive steps.

Eric Siegel is a leading consultant and former Columbia University professor who makes machine learning understandable and captivating. He is the founder of the long-running Predictive Analytics World and the Deep Learning World conference series and is the instructor of Machine Learning for Everyone, a Coursera specialization. He's a popular speaker who has been commissioned for more than 100 keynote addresses, and executive editor of *The Machine Learning Times*. He authored the bestselling *Predictive Analytics: The Power to Predict Who Will Click, Buy, Lie, or Die.*

CHAPTER 7

Assembling Your AI Operations Team

by Terence Tse, Mark Esposito, Takaaki Mizuno, and Danny Goh

Here is a common story of how companies trying to adopt AI fail. They work closely with a promising technology vendor. They invest the time, money, and effort necessary to achieve resounding success with their proof of concept and demonstrate how the use of artificial intelligence will improve their business. Then everything comes to a screeching halt—the companies finds themselves stuck, at a dead end, with their

---

Adapted from "The Dumb Reason Your AI Project Will Fail," on hbr.org, June 8, 2020 (product #H05O4O).

outstanding proof of concept mothballed and their teams frustrated.

What explains the disappointing end? Well, it's hard—in fact, very hard—to *integrate* AI models into a company's overall technology architecture. Doing so requires properly embedding the new technology into the larger IT systems and infrastructure—a top-notch AI won't do you any good if you can't connect it to your existing systems. But while companies pour time and resources into thinking about the AI models themselves, they often do so while failing to consider how to make these models actually work with the systems they have.

The missing component here is AI operations—or "AIOps" for short. This is a practice involving building, integrating, testing, releasing, deploying, and managing the system to turn the results from AI models into the insights desired by the end users. At its most basic, AIOps boils down to having not just the right hardware and software but also the right team: developers and engineers with the skills and knowledge to integrate AI into existing company processes and systems. Evolved from a software engineering and practice that aims to integrate software development and software operations, it is the key to converting the work of AI engines into real business offerings and achieving AI at a large, reliable scale.

Start with the Right Environment

Only a fraction of the code in many AI-powered businesses is devoted to AI functionality—actual AI models are, in reality, a small part of a much larger system, and how users can interface with them matter as much as the model itself. To unlock the value of AI, you need to start with a well-designed production environment (the developers' name for the real-world setting where the code meets the user). Thinking about this design from the beginning will help you manage your project, from probing whether the AI solution can be developed and integrated into the client's IT environment to the integration and deployment of the algorithm in the client's operating system. You want a setting in which software and hardware work seamlessly together, so a business can rely on it to run its real-time daily commercial operations.

A good product environment must successfully meet three criteria:

Dependability

Right now, AI technologies are fraught with technical issues. For example, AI-driven systems and models will stop functioning when fed wrong or malformed data. Furthermore, the speed they can run at is bound to diminish when they have to ingest a large amount of data. These problems will, at best, slow the entire system down and, at worst, bring it to its knees.

Avoiding data bottlenecks is important to creating a dependable environment. Putting well-considered processing and storage architectures in place can overcome throughput and latency issues. Furthermore, anticipation is key. A good AIOps team will consider ways to prevent the environment from crashing and prepare contingency plans for when things do go wrong.

Flexibility

Business objectives—and the supporting flows and processes within the overall system—change on an ongoing basis. At the same time, everything needs to run like clockwork at a system level to enable the AI models to deliver their promised benefits: Data imports must happen at regular intervals according to some fixed rules, reporting mechanisms must be continuously updated, and stale data must be avoided by frequent refreshing.

To meet the ever-evolving business requirements, a production environment needs to be flexible enough for quick and smooth system reconfiguration and data synchronization without compromising running efficiency. Think through how to best build a flexible architecture by breaking it down into manageable chunks, like Lego blocks that can subsequently be added, replaced, or taken off.

Scalability and extendibility

When businesses expand, the "plumbing" within the infrastructure inevitably has to adapt. This can involve scaling up existing capabilities and extending into new competencies. Yet an inescapable fact is that different IT systems often carry different performance, scalability, and extendibility characteristics. The result: Many problems will likely arise when businesses try to cross system boundaries.

Being able to simultaneously retain "business as usual" while embedding upgraded AI models is critical to business expansion. The success depends greatly on the ability of the team to constantly adjust, tinker, and test the existing system with the new proposed solution, reaching equilibrium through functionality of old with new systems.

Good Systems Come from Good Teams

The question, therefore, isn't whether you need an AIOps team, it's what kind of AIOps team makes the most sense for your business. For most businesses, the most important decision they'll make with their AIOps team is whether they want to build the team in house or contract it out. There are advantages to both, but here's what the tradeoffs look like:

Do it yourself

On the plus side, creating your own team to build and maintain a production environment gives you full control over the entire setup. It can also save a lot of potential management and contractual hassles resulting from having to work with external suppliers. This applies to both large companies, which may want to verticalize the AIOps team, as well as for small- to medium-sized enterprises that may want to expand the competencies of their IT team to be able to deal with the production environment directly.

That said, DIY is no small undertaking—it involves significant administrative and organizational burdens, not to mention overhead. Additionally, companies need to develop expertise and knowledge of AIOps in house. The upfront economic impact is also likely to be huge:

High initial cash outlays are needed and tied up to buy depreciating assets like storage hardware and servers. Even with cloud infrastructure, the "trial and error" setup activities will likely push installation costs up.

Plug and play

An alternative is to partner with an AIOps vendor. A good vendor will be able to work closely with its client, offering the required expertise to construct and run a production environment that sits well within the client's IT infrastructure and can support AI models, be they self-developed or supplied by third parties. With such a service, enterprises can access a robust production environment and a trustworthy AIOps team while freeing up the enormous resources otherwise necessary to run their own AIOps.

However, for many businesses, this may mean losing the right to own a proprietary system and a full say in the running of AIOps. It may come across as a compromise between financial constraints and access to a solid and robust AI architecture, which may not be as bespoke as in the case of a native AIOps project but good enough to help the firm digitize its production.

For any business wanting to leverage the benefits of AI, what truly matters is not the AI models themselves; rather, it's the well-oiled machine, powered by AI, that takes the company from where it is today to where it wants to be in the future. Ideals and one-time projects don't. AIOps is therefore not an afterthought; it's a competitive necessity.

Terence Tse is a cofounder of the AI solutions provider Nexus FrontierTech and professor in entrepreneurship at ESCP Business School. **Mark Esposito** is a cofounder and the Chief Learning Officer at Nexus FrontierTech. He has worked as a professor of economics at Hult International Business School and Arizona State University's Thunderbird and served as an institute council coleader for the MOC Program at Harvard Business School. **Takaaki Mizuno** is a cofounder and the CTO at Nexus FrontierTech and the author of numerous publications, including *Web API: The Good Parts*, which became a bestseller on Amazon Japan. **Danny Goh** is a cofounder and the CEO at Nexus FrontierTech and an entrepreneurship expert at the Saïd Business School, University of Oxford.

SECTION THREE

Picking the Right Projects

CHAPTER 8

How to Spot a Machine Learning Opportunity

by Kathryn Hume

The average company faces many challenges in getting started with machine learning, including a shortage of data scientists. But just as important is a shortage of executives and nontechnical employees able to spot AI opportunities. And spotting those opportunities doesn't require a PhD in statistics or even the ability to write code. (It will, spoiler alert, require a brief trip back to high school algebra.)

Adapted from content posted on hbr.org, October 20, 2017 (product #H03Z0H).

Having an intuition for how machine learning algorithms work—even in the most general sense—is becoming an important business skill. Machine learning scientists can't work in a vacuum; business stakeholders should help them identify problems worth solving and allocate subject matter experts to distill their knowledge into labels for data sets, provide feedback on output, and set the objectives for algorithmic success.

As Andrew Ng has written: "Almost all of AI's recent progress is through one type, in which some input data (A) is used to quickly generate some simple response (B)."[1]

But how does this work? Think back to high school math—I promise this will be brief—when you first learned the equation for a straight line: $y = mx + b$. Algebraic equations like this represent the relationship between two variables, x and y. In high school algebra, you'd be told what m and b are, be given an input value for x, and then be asked to plug them into the equation to solve for y. In this case, you start with the equation and then calculate particular values.

Supervised learning reverses this process, solving for m and b, given a set of x's and y's. In supervised learning, you start with many particulars—the data—and infer the general equation. And the learning part means you can update the equation as you see more x's and y's, changing the slope of the line to better fit the data. The equation almost never identifies the relationship between each x and y with 100% accuracy, but the generalization is powerful because later on you can use it to do algebra on new data. Once you've found a slope that captures a relationship between x and y reliably, if you are given a new x value, you can make an educated guess about the corresponding value of y.

As you might imagine, many exciting machine learning problems can't be reduced to a simple equation like $y = mx + b$. But at their essence, supervised machine learning algorithms are also solving for complex versions of m, based on labeled values for x and y, so they can predict future y's from future x's. If you've ever taken a statistics course or worked with predictive analytics, this should all sound familiar: It's the idea behind linear regression, one of the simpler forms of supervised learning.

To return to Ng's formulation, supervised learning requires you to have examples of both the input data and the response, both the x's and the y's. If you have both of those, supervised learning lets you come up with an equation that approximates that relationship, so in the future you can guess y values for any new value of x.

So the question of how to identify AI opportunities starts with asking: What are some outcomes worth guessing? And do we have the data necessary to do supervised learning?

For example, let's say a data scientist is tasked with predicting real estate prices for a neighborhood. After analyzing the data, she finds that housing price (y) is tightly correlated to size of house (x). So, she'd use many data points containing both houses' size and price, use statistics to estimate the slope (m), and then use the equation $y = mx + b$ to predict the price for a given house based on its size. This is linear regression, and it remains incredibly powerful.

Organizations use similar techniques to predict future product sales, investment portfolio risk, or customer churn. Again, the statistics behind different algorithms vary in complexity. Some techniques output simple point predictions (We think y will happen!), and others output a range of possible predictions with affiliated confidence rates (There's a 70% chance y will happen, but if we change one assumption, our confidence falls to 60%).

These are all examples of prediction problems, but supervised learning is also used for classification.

Classification tasks clump data into buckets. Here a data scientist looks for features in data that are reliable proxies for categories she wants to separate: If data has feature x, it goes into bucket one; if not, it goes into bucket two. You can still think of this as using x's to predict y's, but in this case, y isn't a number but a type.

Organizations use classification algorithms to filter spam, diagnose abnormalities on X-rays, identify relevant documents for a lawsuit, sort résumés for a job, or segment customers. But classification gains its true power when the number of classes increases. Classification can be extended beyond binary choices like "Is it spam or not?" to include lots of different buckets. Perception tasks, like training a computer to recognize objects in images, are also classification tasks: They just have many output classes (for example, the various animal species names) instead of just bucket 1 and bucket 2. This makes supervised learning systems look smarter than they are, as we assume their ability to learn concepts mirrors our own. In fact, they're just bucketing data into buckets 1, 2, 3... n, according to the m learned for the function.

So far, this all feels rather abstract. How can you bring it down to earth and learn how to identify these mathematical structures in your everyday work?

There are a few ways you can determine whether a task presents a good supervised-learning opportunity.

Write down what you do in your job

Break apart your activities into:

- Things you do daily or regularly versus things you do sporadically

- Things that have become second nature versus things that require patient deliberation or lots of thought

- Things that are part of a process versus things you do on your own

Examine the task

For those tasks that you perform regularly on your own and that feel automatic, identify how many others in your organization do similar tasks and how many people have done such tasks historically. Do these tasks include predicting something or bucketing something into categories?

Ask yourself: If 10 colleagues in your organization performed such a task, would they all agree on the answer? If humans can't agree something is true or false, computers can't reliably transform judgment calls into statistical patterns.

How long have people in the organization been doing something similar to this task? If it's been a long time, has the organization kept a record of successfully completed tasks? If yes, this could be used as a training data set for your supervised-learning algorithm. If no, you may need to start collecting this data today, and then you can keep a human in the loop to train the algorithm over time.

Talk to your data science team about the task

Walk team members through your thought process and tell them what aspects of information you focus on when you complete your task. This will help them determine if automation is feasible and tease out the aspects of the data that will be most predictive of the desired output.

Think about potential outcomes

Ask yourself, if this were automated, how might that change the products we offer to our customers? What is the worst thing that could happen to the business if this were to be automated? And finally, what is the worst thing that could happen to the business if the algorithm outputs the wrong answer or an answer with a 65% or 70% accuracy rate? What is the accuracy threshold the business requires to go ahead and automate this task?

Succeeding with supervised learning entails a shift in the perspective on how work gets done. It entails using past work—all that human judgment and subject matter expertise—to create an algorithm that applies that expertise to future work. When used well, this makes employees more productive and creates new value. But it starts with identifying problems worth solving and thinking about them in terms of inputs and outputs, x's and y's.

Kathryn Hume is the Vice President of Digital Investments Technology at the Royal Bank of Canada. Prior to joining RBC, Hume held leadership positions at Integrate.ai and Fast Forward Labs, where she helped over 50 *Fortune* 500 organizations develop and implement AI programs. She has taught courses on digital transformation and legal ethics at the business and law schools at Harvard, MIT, the University of Toronto, and the University of Calgary.

NOTE

1. Andrew Ng, "What Artificial Intelligence Can and Can't Do Right Now," November 9, 2016, https://hbr.org/2016/11/what-artificial-intelligence-can-and-cant-do-right-now.

CHAPTER 9

A Simple Tool to Start Making Decisions with the Help of AI

by Ajay Agrawal, Joshua Gans, and Avi Goldfarb

There is no shortage of hot takes regarding the significant impact that AI is going to have on business in the near future. Much less has been written about how, exactly, companies should get started with it. In our research, we begin by distilling AI down to its very simplest economics, and we offer one approach to taking that first step.

Adapted from content posted on hbr.org, April 17, 2018 (product #H04ABS).

Picking the Right Projects

We start with a simple insight: Recent developments in AI are about lowering the cost of prediction. AI makes prediction better, faster, and cheaper. Not only can you more easily predict the future (What's the weather going to be like next week?), but you can also predict the present (what is the English translation of this Spanish website?). Prediction is about using information you have to generate information you don't have. Anywhere you have lots of information (data) and want to filter, squeeze, or sort it into insights that will facilitate decision-making, prediction will help get that done. And now machines can do it.

Better predictions matter when you make decisions in the face of uncertainty, as every business does, constantly. But how do you think through what it would take to incorporate a prediction machine into your decision-making process?

In teaching this subject to MBA graduates at the University of Toronto's Rotman School of Management, we have introduced a simple decision-making tool: the AI Canvas (see figure 9-1). Each space on the canvas contains one of the requirements for machine-assisted decision-making, beginning with a prediction.

To explain how the AI Canvas works, we'll use a real example crafted during one of our AI strategy workshops by Craig Campbell, former CEO of Peloton Innovations (now called RSPNDR) a venture tackling the security industry with AI (see figure 9-2).

Over 97% of the time that a home security alarm goes off, it's a false alarm. That is, something other than an

FIGURE 9-1

The AI Canvas

Use this tool to think through how AI could help with business decisions.

Prediction	Judgment	Action	Outcome
What do you need to know to make the decision?	How do you value different outcomes and errors?	What are you trying to do?	What are your metrics for task success?

Input	Training	Feedback
What data do you need to run the predictive algorithm?	What data do you need to train the predictive algorithm?	How can you use the outcomes to improve the algorithm?

unknown intruder (threat) triggered it. This requires security companies to make a decision as to what to do: Dispatch police or a guard? Phone the homeowner? Ignore it? If the security company decides to take action, more than 90 out of 100 times, it will turn out that the action was wasted. However, always taking an action in response to an alarm signal means that when a threat is indeed present, the security company responds.

How can you decide whether employing a prediction machine will improve matters? The AI Canvas is a simple tool that helps you organize what you need to know into seven categories in order to systematically make that assessment. We provide an example for the security alarm case.

First, you specify what you are trying to *predict*. In the alarm case, you want to know whether an alarm is caused by an unknown person or not (true versus false alarm). A prediction machine can potentially tell you this—after all, an alarm with a simple movement sensor is already a sort of prediction machine. With machine learning, you can take a richer range of sensor inputs to determine what you really want to predict: whether the movement was caused specifically by an unknown person. With the right sensors—say, a camera in the home to identify known faces or pets, a door key that recognizes when someone is present, and so on—today's AI techniques can provide a more nuanced prediction. The prediction is no longer "movement = alarm" but, for example, "movement + unrecognized face = alarm." This more sophisticated prediction reduces the number of false

FIGURE 9-2

The AI Canvas: An example using AI to improve home security

Prediction	Judgment	Action	Outcome
Predict whether an alarm is caused by an unknown person vs. something else (i.e., true vs. false).	Compare the cost of responding to a false alarm to the cost of not responding to a true alarm.	Dispatch a security response or not when an alarm is triggered.	Observe whether the action taken in response to the triggered alarm was correct.

Input	Training	Feedback
Sensor inputs from movement, heat, camera, and contextual data at each point in time when the alarm is on; these data are used to operate the AI.	Historical sensor data matched with historical outcome data (actual intruder vs. false alarm); these data are used to train the AI before it is deployed.	Sensor data matched with data collected from outcomes (verified intruders vs. verified false alarms); these data are used to update the model, continuously improving the AI while it is operating.

alarms, making the decision to send a response, as opposed to trying to contact the owner first, an easier one.

No prediction is 100% accurate. So, in order to determine the value of investing in better prediction, you need to know the cost of a false alarm, as compared with the cost of dismissing an alarm when it is true. This will depend on the situation and requires human *judgment*. How costly is a response phone call to verify what is happening? How expensive is it to dispatch a security guard in response to an alarm? How much is it worth to respond quickly? How costly is it to not respond if it turns out that there was an intruder in the home? There are many factors to consider; determining their relative weights requires judgment.

Such judgment can change the nature of the prediction machine you deploy. In the alarm case, having cameras all over the house may be the best way of determining the presence of an unknown intruder. But many people will be uncomfortable with this. Some people would prefer to trade the cost of dealing with more false alarms for enhanced privacy. Judgment sometimes requires determining the relative value of factors that are difficult to quantify and thus compare. While the cost of false alarms may be easy to quantify, the value of privacy is not.

Next, you identify the *action* that is dependent on the predictions generated. This may be a simple "dispatch/don't dispatch" decision, or it may be more nuanced. Perhaps the options for action include not just dispatching someone but also enabling immediate remote monitoring of who is in the home or some form of contact with the homeowner.

An action leads to an *outcome*. For example, the security company dispatched a security guard (action), and the guard discovered an intruder (outcome). In other words, looking back, we are able to see for each decision whether the right response occurred. Knowing this is important for evaluating whether there is scope to improve predictions over time. If you do not know what outcome you want, improvement is difficult, if not impossible.

The top row of the canvas—prediction, judgment, action, and outcome—describes the critical aspects of a decision. On the bottom row of the canvas are three final considerations. They all relate to data. To generate a useful prediction, you need to know what is going on at the time a decision needs to be made—in this case, when an alarm is triggered. In our example, this includes motion data and image data collected at the home in real time. That is your basic *input* data.

But to develop the prediction machine in the first place, you need to train a machine learning model. *Training* data matches historical sensor data with prior outcomes to calibrate the algorithms at the heart of the prediction machine. In this case, imagine a giant spreadsheet where each row is a time the alarm went off, whether there was in fact an intruder, and a bunch of other data like time of day and location. The richer and more varied that training data, the better your predictions will be out of the gate. If that data is not available, then you might have to deploy a mediocre prediction machine and wait for it to improve over time.

Those improvements come from *feedback* data. This is data that you collect when the prediction machine is operating in real situations. Feedback data is often generated from a richer set of environments than training data. In our example, you may correlate outcomes with data collected from sensors through windows, which affect how movements are detected, and how cameras capture a facial image—perhaps more realistic than the data used for training. So, you can improve the accuracy of predictions further with continual training using feedback data. Sometimes feedback data will be tailored to an individual home. Other times, it might aggregate data from many homes.

Clarifying these seven factors for each critical decision throughout your organization will help you get started on identifying opportunities for AIs to either reduce costs or enhance performance. Here we discussed a decision associated with a specific situation. To get started with AI, your challenge is to identify the key decisions in your organization where the outcome hinges on uncertainty. Filling out the AI Canvas won't tell you whether you should make your own AI or buy one from a vendor, but it will help you clarify what the AI will contribute (the prediction), how it will interface with humans (judgment), how it will be used to influence decisions (action), how you will measure success (outcome), and the types of data that will be required to train, operate, and improve the AI.

The potential is enormous. For example, alarms communicate predictions to a remote agent. Part of the reason for this approach is that there are so many false signals. But just think: If our prediction machine became so good that there were no false alarms, then is dispatch still the right response? One can imagine alternative responses, such as an on-site intruder capture system (as in cartoons!), which could be more feasible with significantly more accurate and high-fidelity predictions. More generally, better predictions will create opportunities for entirely new ways to approach security, potentially predicting the intent of intruders before they even enter.

Ajay Agrawal is the Geoffrey Taber Chair in Entrepreneurship and Innovation at the University of Toronto's Rotman School of Management. He is the founder of the Creative Destruction Lab, cofounder of The Next AI, and cofounder of Kindred. **Joshua Gans** is the Jeffrey S. Skoll Chair in Technical Innovation and Entrepreneurship at the Rotman School of Management, University of Toronto, and the chief economist at the Creative Destruction Lab. **Avi Goldfarb** is the Rotman Chair in Artificial Intelligence and Healthcare at the Rotman School of Management, University of Toronto. He is also the chief data scientist at the Creative Destruction Lab. Agrawal, Gans, and Goldfarb are the coauthors of *Power and Prediction: The Disruptive Economics of Artificial Intelligence* (Harvard Business Review Press, 2022) and *Prediction Machines: The Simple Economics of Artificial Intelligence* (Harvard Business Review Press, 2018).

CHAPTER 10

How to Pick the Right Automation Project

by Bhaskar Ghosh, Rajendra Prasad, and Gayathri Pallail

Whenever a new wave of technology splashes onto the scene, managers face the same questions: Where do we start applying it first? Do we go after the low-hanging fruit that will produce quick wins and build the case for more ambitious projects? Or should we strategically focus, with no delay, on the applications that will give us a decisive edge over competitors?

Adapted from content posted on hbr.org, February 10, 2022 (product #H06UWZ).

Right now, with the arrival of a revolutionary set of technologies for automating knowledge work—artificial intelligence in particular—we see teams grappling with these questions at high levels in organizations. So, where should you start?

Instead of framing your goals in terms of quick victories (which won't really move the needle) or major strategic applications (which require skills and foundations you don't yet have in place), focus on how your first steps will build capabilities in your organization. You should sequence the projects you take on—knowing you will ultimately take on hundreds—so that the early ones *build the AI talents* and *put in place the AI tech infrastructure* for the projects you will take on next, and next, and next.

Map Where You Want to Go

Capability-building—developing the strength of an organization to solve a class of problems it will keep facing in the future—is a challenge you might have tackled in other realms. In areas from strategy formulation to project management, teams recognize that they can and must get better by learning from experience. And because there are fundamentals that must be mastered before they can advance to higher-order capabilities, teams often take their guidance from so-called *maturity models*, outlined by experts who have watched others travel the same path before. Given that your people will need to rise again and again to the challenge of implementing intelligent automation solutions, this is the approach that makes sense, but more of the thinking about the best sequence of steps will be up to you.

Planning this journey requires mapping out how your team or organization will deliberately move from a state of being a novice to being an expert.

Assess your existing capabilities

Tease out the challenges your people already know how to tackle and the sophistication of the tools they have to solve them. Perhaps you already have strong data analytics skills on staff, for example, or people who have been involved in robotic process automation installations elsewhere.

Perform gap analysis

This details the difference between your current capabilities and the demands of the most challenging solution you can envision taking on. This might reveal that your current IT infrastructure is simply not equal to a coming wave of applications that it will need to interact with disparate data sources. Or that much more effective collaboration will be needed between software developers and business process owners than has been seen in the past.

Sequence your projects

Finally, with the beginning and end states clearly articulated, you can then specify a step-by-step journey, with projects sequenced according to which ones can do the most early on to lay essential foundations for later initiatives.

Case Study: Automation at a Construction Equipment Manufacturer

Here's an example to illustrate how this approach can lead to better choices. At a construction equipment manufacturer, there are three tempting areas to automate. One is the solution a vendor is offering: a chatbot tool that can be fairly simply implemented in the internal IT help desk with immediate impact on wait times and head count. A second possibility is in finance, where sales forecasting could be enhanced by predictive modeling boosted by AI pattern recognition. The third idea is a big one: If the company could use intelligent automation to create a "connected equipment" environment on customer job sites, its business model could shift to new revenue streams from digital services such as monitoring and controlling machinery remotely.

If you're going for a relatively easy implementation and fast ROI, the first option is a no-brainer. If instead you're looking for big publicity for your organization's bold new vision, the third one's the ticket. You can set up a tiger team or separate organization and give it full license to disrupt the existing business. But note that neither of those approaches really prepares the ground for intelligent automation to spread to other applications by the existing organization; they don't make the people of your organization generally more interested, receptive, or able to apply intelligent technology elsewhere. In other words, as an organization, taking these routes doesn't take you far up the learning curve toward greater maturity with the technology.

This is what option two would do—in large part because it would demand that the company get its act together on data. Without a good enterprise data strategy, people in different parts of the organization lack common standards regarding what data needs to be gathered and how it should be organized, cleaned, and prepped for analysis. This is a foundational capability that the company will need to have in place to make headway in using machine learning at scale. From the standpoint of capability-building, it is easy to see how progress on enterprise data would unlock, say, 10 other projects—which in turn can be prioritized by the further capabilities they could add. Our manufacturing company could lay out a roadmap showing how, five years later, it will not only be reaping the returns of the specific projects, but also be generally and profoundly more ready to take on truly transformative initiatives.

Bhaskar Ghosh is Accenture's Chief Strategy Officer and a member of the firm's Global Management Committee. **Rajendra Prasad** is Global Automation Lead at Accenture. A holder of multiple patents, he also built the firm's AI-powered intelligent automation platform for use in client engagements. **Gayathri Pallail** is a managing director and oversees automation strategy and deployment at Accenture and has implemented solutions in over 500 client organizations across industries and sectors. Ghosh, Prasad, and Pallail are the coauthors of *The Automation Advantage: Embrace the Future of Productivity and Improve Speed, Quality, and Customer Experience Through AI.*

SECTION FOUR

Working with AI

CHAPTER 11

Collaborative Intelligence: Humans and AI Are Joining Forces

by H. James Wilson and Paul Daugherty

Artificial intelligence is becoming good at many "human" jobs—diagnosing disease, translating languages, providing customer service—and it's improving fast. This is raising reasonable fears that AI will ultimately replace

---

Adapted from an article in *Harvard Business Review*, July–August 2018 (product #R1804J).

human workers throughout the economy. But that's not the inevitable, or even most likely, outcome. Never before have digital tools been so responsive to us, nor we to our tools. While AI will radically alter how work gets done and who does it, the technology's larger impact will be in complementing and augmenting human capabilities, not replacing them.

Certainly, many companies have used AI to automate processes, but those that deploy it mainly to displace employees will see only short-term productivity gains. In our research involving 1,500 companies, we found that firms achieve the most significant performance improvements when humans and machines work together. Through such collaborative intelligence, humans and AI actively enhance each other's complementary strengths: the leadership, teamwork, creativity, and social skills of the former and the speed, scalability, and quantitative capabilities of the latter. What comes naturally to people (making a joke, for example) can be tricky for machines, and what's straightforward for machines (analyzing gigabytes of data) remains virtually impossible for humans. Business requires both kinds of capabilities.

To take full advantage of this collaboration, companies must understand how humans can most effectively augment machines, how machines can enhance what humans do best, and how to redesign business processes to support the partnership. Through our research and work in the field, we have developed guidelines to help companies achieve this and put the power of collaborative intelligence to work.

Humans Assisting Machines

Humans need to perform three crucial roles. They must *train* machines to perform certain tasks; *explain* the outcomes of those tasks, especially when the results are counterintuitive or controversial; and *sustain* the responsible use of machines (by, for example, preventing robots from harming humans).

Training

Machine learning algorithms must be taught how to perform the work they're designed to do. In that effort, huge training data sets are amassed to teach machine-translation apps to handle idiomatic expressions, medical apps to detect disease, and recommendation engines to support financial decision-making. In addition, AI systems must be trained how best to interact with humans. While organizations across sectors are now in the early stages of filling trainer roles, leading tech companies and research groups already have mature training staffs and expertise.

Consider Microsoft's AI assistant, Cortana. The bot required extensive training to develop just the right personality: confident, caring, and helpful but not bossy. Instilling those qualities took countless hours of attention by a team that included a poet, a novelist, and a playwright. Similarly, human trainers were needed to develop the personalities of Apple's Siri and Amazon's Alexa to ensure that they accurately reflected their companies' brands. Siri, for example, has just a touch of sassiness, as consumers might expect from Apple.

AI assistants are now being trained to display even more complex and subtle human traits, such as sympathy. The startup Koko, an offshoot of the MIT Media Lab, has developed technology that can help AI assistants seem to commiserate. For instance, if a user is having a bad day, the Koko system doesn't reply with a canned response such as "I'm sorry to hear that." Instead it may ask for more information and then offer advice to help the person see his issues in a different light. If he were feeling stressed, for instance, Koko might recommend thinking of that tension as a positive emotion that could be channeled into action.

Explaining

As AIs increasingly reach conclusions through processes that are opaque (the so-called black-box problem), they require human experts in the field to explain their behavior to nonexpert users. These "explainers" are particularly important in evidence-based industries, such as law and medicine, where a practitioner needs to understand how an AI weighed inputs into, say, a sentencing or medical recommendation. Explainers are similarly important in helping insurers and law enforcement understand why an autonomous car took actions that led to an accident—or failed to avoid one. And explainers are becoming integral in regulated industries—indeed, in any consumer-facing industry where a machine's output could be challenged as unfair, illegal, or just plain wrong. For instance, the European Union's new General Data Protection Regulation (GDPR) gives consumers the right to receive an explanation for any algorithm-based decision, such as the rate offer on a credit card or mortgage. This is one area where AI will contribute to *increased* employment: Experts estimate that companies will have to create about 75,000 new jobs to administer the GDPR requirements.

Sustaining

In addition to having people who can explain AI outcomes, companies need "sustainers"—employees who continually work to ensure that AI systems are functioning properly, safely, and responsibly.

For example, an array of experts sometimes referred to as safety engineers focus on anticipating and trying to prevent harm by AIs. The developers of industrial robots that work alongside people have paid careful attention to ensuring that they recognize humans nearby and don't endanger them. These experts may also review analysis from explainers when AIs do cause harm, as when a self-driving car is involved in a fatal accident.

Other groups of sustainers make sure that AI systems uphold ethical norms. If an AI system for credit approval, for example, is found to be discriminating against people in certain groups (as has happened), these ethics managers are responsible for investigating and addressing the problem. Playing a similar role, data compliance officers try to ensure that the data that is feeding AI systems complies with the GDPR and other consumer-protection regulations. A related data-use role involves ensuring that AIs manage information responsibly. Like many tech companies, Apple uses AI to collect personal details about users as they engage with the company's devices and software. The aim is to improve the user experience, but unconstrained data gathering can compromise privacy, anger customers, and run afoul of the law. The company's "differential privacy team" works to make sure that while the AI seeks to learn as much as possible about a group of users in a statistical sense, it is protecting the privacy of individual users.

Machines Assisting Humans

Smart machines are helping humans expand their abilities in three ways. They can *amplify* our cognitive strengths, *interact* with customers and employees to free us for higher-level tasks, and *embody* human skills to extend our physical capabilities.

Amplifying

Artificial intelligence can boost our analytic and decision-making abilities by providing the right information at the right time. But it can also heighten creativity. Consider how Autodesk's Dreamcatcher AI enhances the imagination of even exceptional designers. A designer provides Dreamcatcher with criteria about the desired product—for example, a chair able to support up to 300 pounds, with a seat 18 inches off the ground, made of materials costing less than $75, and so on. She can also supply information about other chairs that she finds attractive. Dreamcatcher then churns out thousands of designs that match those criteria, often sparking ideas that the designer might not have initially considered. She can then guide the software, telling it which chairs she likes or doesn't, leading to a new round of designs.

Throughout the iterative process, Dreamcatcher performs the myriad calculations needed to ensure that each proposed design meets the specified criteria. This frees the designer to concentrate on deploying uniquely human strengths: professional judgment and aesthetic sensibilities.

Interacting

Human-machine collaboration enables companies to interact with employees and customers in novel, more effective ways. AI agents like Cortana, for example, can facilitate communications between people or on behalf of people, such as by transcribing a meeting and distributing a voice-searchable version to those who couldn't attend. Such applications are inherently scalable—a single chatbot, for instance, can provide routine customer service to large numbers of people simultaneously, wherever they may be.

SEB, a major Swedish bank, now uses a virtual assistant called Aida to interact with millions of customers. Able to handle natural-language conversations, Aida has access to vast stores of data and can answer many frequently asked questions, such as how to open an account or make cross-border payments. She can also ask callers follow-up questions to solve their problems, and she's able to analyze a caller's tone of voice (frustrated versus appreciative, for instance) and use that information to provide better service later. Whenever the system can't resolve an issue—which happens in about 30% of cases—

it turns the caller over to a human customer-service representative and then monitors that interaction to learn how to resolve similar problems in the future. With Aida handling basic requests, human reps can concentrate on addressing more complex issues, especially those from unhappy callers who might require extra hand-holding.

Embodying

Many AIs, like Aida and Cortana, exist principally as digital entities, but in other applications the intelligence is embodied in a robot that augments a human worker. With their sophisticated sensors, motors, and actuators, AI-enabled machines can now recognize people and objects and work safely alongside humans in factories, warehouses, and laboratories.

In manufacturing, for example, robots are evolving from potentially dangerous and "dumb" industrial machines into smart, context-aware "cobots." A cobot arm might, for example, handle repetitive actions that require heavy lifting, while a person performs complementary tasks that require dexterity and human judgment, such as assembling a gear motor.

Hyundai is extending the cobot concept with exoskeletons. These wearable robotic devices, which adapt to the user and location in real time, will enable industrial workers to perform their jobs with superhuman endurance and strength.

Reimagining Your Business

In order to get the most value from AI, operations need to be redesigned. To do this, companies must first discover and describe an operational area that can be improved. It might be a balky internal process (such as HR's slowness to fill staff positions), or it could be a previously intractable problem that can now be addressed using AI (such as quickly identifying adverse drug reactions across patient populations). Moreover, a number of new AI and advanced analytic techniques can help surface previously invisible problems that are amenable to AI solutions.

Next, companies must develop a solution through cocreation—having stakeholders envision how they might collaborate with AI systems to improve a process. Consider the case of a large agricultural company that wanted to deploy AI technology to help farmers. An enormous amount of data was available about soil properties, weather patterns, historical harvests, and so forth, and the initial plan was to build an AI application that would more accurately predict future crop yields. But in discussions with farmers, the company learned of a more pressing need. What farmers really wanted was a system that could provide real-time recommendations on how to increase productivity—which crops to plant, where to grow them, how much nitrogen to use in the soil, and so on. The company developed an AI system to provide such advice, and the initial outcomes were promising; farmers were happy about the crop yields obtained with the AI's guidance. Results from that initial test were then fed back into the system to refine the algorithms used. As with the discovery step, new AI and analytic techniques can assist in cocreation by suggesting novel approaches to improving processes.

The third step for companies is to scale and then sustain the proposed solution. SEB, for example, originally deployed a version of Aida internally to assist 15,000 bank employees but thereafter rolled out the chatbot to its 1 million customers.

Through our work with hundreds of companies, we have identified five characteristics of business processes that companies typically want to improve: flexibility, speed, scale, decision-making, and personalization. When reimagining a business process, determine which of these characteristics is central to the desired transformation, how intelligent collaboration could be harnessed to address it, and what alignments and trade-offs with other process characteristics will be necessary.

Flexibility

For Mercedes-Benz executives, inflexible processes presented a growing challenge. Increasingly, the company's most profitable customers had been demanding individualized S-class sedans, but the automaker's assembly systems couldn't deliver the customization people wanted.

Traditionally, car manufacturing has been a rigid process with automated steps executed by "dumb" robots. To improve flexibility, Mercedes replaced some of those robots with AI-enabled cobots and redesigned its processes around human-machine collaborations. At the company's plant near Stuttgart, Germany, cobot arms guided by human workers pick up and place heavy parts, becoming an extension of the worker's body. This system puts the worker in control of the build of each car, doing less manual labor and more of a "piloting" job with the robot.

The company's human-machine teams can adapt on the fly. In the plant, the cobots can be reprogrammed easily with a tablet, allowing them to handle different tasks depending on changes in the workflow. Such agility has enabled the manufacturer to achieve unprecedented levels of customization. Mercedes can individualize vehicle production according to the real-time choices consumers make at dealerships, changing everything from a vehicle's dashboard components to the seat leather to the tire valve caps. As a result, no two cars rolling off the assembly line at the Stuttgart plant are the same.

Speed

Some business activities place a premium on speed. One such operation is the detection of credit-card fraud. Companies have just seconds to determine whether they should approve a given transaction. If it's fraudulent, they will most likely have to eat that loss. But if they deny a legitimate transaction, they lose the fee from that purchase and anger the customer.

Like most major banks, HSBC has developed an AI-based solution that improves the speed and accuracy of fraud detection. The AI monitors and scores millions of transactions daily, using data on purchase location and customer behavior, IP addresses, and other information to identify subtle patterns that signal possible fraud. HSBC first implemented the system in the United States, significantly reducing the rate of undetected fraud and false positives, and then rolled it out in the United Kingdom and Asia. A different AI system used by Danske Bank improved its fraud-detection rate by 50% and decreased false positives by 60%. The reduction in the number of false positives frees investigators to concentrate their efforts on equivocal transactions the AI has flagged, where human judgment is needed.

The fight against financial fraud is like an arms race: Better detection leads to more-devious criminals, which leads to better detection, which continues the cycle. Thus the algorithms and scoring models for combating fraud have a very short shelf life and require continual updating. In addition, different countries and regions use different models. For these reasons, legions of data analysts, IT professionals, and experts in financial fraud are needed at the interface between humans and machines to keep the software a step ahead of the criminals.

Scale

For many business processes, poor scalability is the primary obstacle to improvement. That's particularly true of processes that depend on intensive human labor with minimal machine assistance. Consider, for instance, the employee recruitment process at Unilever. The consumer goods giant was looking for a way to diversify its 170,000-person workforce. HR determined that it needed to focus on entry-level hires and then fast-track the best into management. But the company's existing processes weren't able to evaluate potential recruits in sufficient numbers—while giving each applicant individual attention—to ensure a diverse population of exceptional talent.

Here's how Unilever combined human and AI capabilities to scale individualized hiring: In the first round of the application process, candidates are asked to play online games that help assess traits such as risk aversion. These games have no right or wrong answers, but they help Unilever's AI figure out which individuals might be best suited for a particular position. In the next round, applicants are asked to submit a video in which they answer questions designed for the specific position they're interested in. Their responses are analyzed by an AI system that considers not just what they say but also their body language and tone. The best candidates from that round, as judged by the AI, are then invited to Unilever for in-person interviews, after which humans make the final hiring decisions.

It's too early to tell whether the new recruiting process has resulted in better employees. The company has been closely tracking the success of those hires, but more data is still needed. It is clear, however, that the new system has greatly broadened the scale of Unilever's recruiting. In part because job seekers can easily access the system by smartphone, the number of applicants doubled to 30,000 within a year, the number of universities represented surged from 840 to 2,600, and the socioeconomic diversity of new hires increased. Furthermore, the average time from application to hiring decision has dropped from four months to just four weeks, while the time that recruiters spend reviewing applications has fallen by 75%.

Decision-making

By providing employees with tailored information and guidance, AI can help them reach better decisions. This can be especially valuable for workers in the trenches, where making the right call can have a huge impact on the bottom line.

Consider the way in which equipment maintenance is being improved with the use of "digital twins"—virtual models of physical equipment. General Electric builds such software models of its turbines and other industrial products and continually updates them with operating data streaming from the equipment. By collecting readings from large numbers of machines in the field, GE has amassed a wealth of information on normal and aberrant performance. Its Predix application, which uses machine learning algorithms, can now predict when a specific part in an individual machine might fail.

This technology has fundamentally changed the decision-intensive process of maintaining industrial equipment. Predix might, for example, identify some unexpected rotor wear and tear in a turbine, check the turbine's operational history, report that the damage has increased fourfold over the past few months, and warn that if nothing is done, the rotor will lose an estimated 70% of its useful life. The system can then suggest appropriate actions, taking into account the machine's current condition, the operating environment, and aggregated data about similar damage and repairs to other machines. Along with its recommendations, Predix can generate information about their costs and financial benefits and provide a confidence level (say, 95%) for the assumptions used in its analysis.

Without Predix, workers would be lucky to catch the rotor damage on a routine maintenance check. It's possible that it would go undetected until the rotor failed, resulting in a costly shutdown. With Predix, maintenance workers are alerted to potential problems before they become serious, and they have the needed information at their fingertips to make good decisions—ones that can sometimes save GE millions of dollars.

Personalization

Providing customers with individually tailored brand experiences is the holy grail of marketing. With AI, such personalization can now be achieved with previously unimaginable precision and at vast scale. Think of the way the music streaming service Pandora uses AI algorithms to generate personalized playlists for each of its millions of users according to their preferences in songs, artists, and genres. Or consider Starbucks, which, with customers' permission, uses AI to recognize their mobile devices and call up their ordering history to help baristas make serving recommendations. The AI technology does what it does best, sifting through and processing copious amounts of data to recommend certain offerings or actions, and humans do what they do best, exercising their intuition and judgment to make a recommendation or select the best fit from a set of choices.

The Carnival Corporation is applying AI to personalize the cruise experience for millions of vacationers through a wearable device called the Ocean Medallion

FIVE SCHOOLS OF THOUGHT ON AI AND THE FUTURE OF WORK

by Mark Knickrehm

It's abundantly clear that AI, big data analytics, and advanced robotics make it possible for machines to take on tasks that once required a person. How should companies prepare, strategically, to thrive in this world?

Views on what to expect vary dramatically. It's critical to understand the range of opinions on this issue, because implicitly or explicitly, they will influence the way business leaders create the workforce of the future.

The Dystopians

Humans and machines will wage a Darwinian struggle that machines will win. AI systems will take on tasks at the heart of middle- and high-skill jobs, while robots will perform menial work that requires low-skill labor. The result will be massive unemployment, falling wages, and wrenching economic dislocation. Falling incomes will have grave consequences in advanced economies.

The Utopians

Intelligent machines will take on even more work, and the result will be unprecedented wealth. AI and computing power will advance in the next two decades to achieve "the singularity"—when machines will be able to emulate the workings of the human brain in its entirety. Human brains will be "scanned" and "downloaded" to computers and billions of replicated human brains will do most of the cognitive work, while robots will do all the heavy lifting. Economic output could double every three months. The singularity may even lead to a world where little human labor is required, a universal income program covers basic needs, and people apply their talents to meaningful pursuits.

The Technology Optimists

A burst of productivity has already begun but is not captured in official data. When companies do take full advantage of intelligent technologies, a leap in productivity will create both economic growth and improvements in living standards. However, the bounty won't be distributed evenly, and many jobs will be displaced.

The Productivity Skeptics

Despite the power of intelligent technologies, any gains in national productivity levels will be low. Combine that with headwinds from aging populations, income inequality, and the costs of dealing with climate change, and advanced economies will have near-zero GDP growth.

The Optimistic Realists

Intelligent machines can spur productivity gains that match previous technology waves. Productivity will advance rapidly in certain sectors and for high-performing companies. New jobs will be created, but intelligent technologies may exacerbate the trends of the recent past, in which demand rose for both high- and low-skill workers whose jobs could not be automated easily, while demand for middle-skill workers fell.

Mark Knickrehm is group chief executive for Accenture Strategy.

Adapted from "How Will AI Change Work? Here Are 5 Schools of Thought" on hbr.org, January 24, 2018 (product #H0449F).

and a network that allows smart devices to connect. Machine learning dynamically processes the data flowing from the medallion and from sensors and systems throughout the ship to help guests get the most out of their vacations. The medallion streamlines the boarding and debarking processes, tracks the guests' activities, simplifies purchasing by connecting their credit cards to the device, and acts as a room key. It also connects to a system that anticipates guests' preferences, helping crew members deliver personalized service to each guest by suggesting tailored itineraries of activities and dining experiences.

The Need for New Roles and Talent

Reimagining a business process involves more than the implementation of AI technology; it also requires a significant commitment to developing employees with what we call "fusion skills"—those that enable them to work effectively at the human-machine interface. To start, people must learn to delegate tasks to the new technology, as when physicians trust computers to help read X-rays and MRIs. Employees should also know how to combine their distinctive human skills with those of a smart machine to get a better outcome than either could achieve alone, as in robot-assisted surgery. Workers must be able to teach intelligent agents new skills and undergo training to work well within AI-enhanced processes. For example, they must know how best to put questions to an AI agent to get the information they need. And there must be employees, like those on Apple's differential privacy team, who ensure that their companies' AI systems are used responsibly and not for illegal or unethical purposes.

We expect that in the future, company roles will be redesigned around the desired outcomes of reimagined processes, and corporations will increasingly be organized around different types of skills rather than around rigid job titles. AT&T has already begun that transition as it shifts from landline telephone services to mobile networks and starts to retrain 100,000 employees for new positions. As part of that effort, the company has completely overhauled its organizational chart: Approximately 2,000 job titles have been streamlined into a much smaller number of broad categories encompassing similar skills. Some of those skills are what one might expect (for example, proficiency in data science and data wrangling), while others are less obvious (for instance, the ability to use simple machine learning tools to cross-sell services).

Conclusion

Most activities at the human-machine interface require people to *do new and different things* (such as train a chatbot) and to *do things differently* (use that chatbot to provide better customer service). So far, however, only a small number of the companies we've surveyed have begun to reimagine their business processes to optimize collaborative intelligence. But the lesson is clear: Organizations that use machines merely to displace workers through automation will miss the full potential of AI. Such a strategy is misguided from the get-go. Tomorrow's leaders will instead be those who embrace collaborative intelligence, transforming their operations, their markets, their industries, and—no less important—their workforces.

———————

H. James Wilson is the global managing director of thought leadership and technology research at Accenture. **Paul Daugherty** is Accenture's group chief executive—technology and CTO. Wilson and Daugherty are coauthors of *Radically Human: How New Technology Is Transforming Business and Shaping Our Future* (Harvard Business Review Press, 2022) and *Human + Machine: Reimagining Work in the Age of AI* (Harvard Business Review Press, 2018).

CHAPTER 12

How to Get Employees to Embrace AI

by Brad Power

David Maister was angry. He had been surprised and annoyed to learn that his company had set up a new AI-based marketing system that was doing most of what he thought was his job as digital marketing manager at Global Consumer Brands: deciding what ads to place where, for which customer segments, and how much to spend. And when he found that the system was buying ads for audiences that didn't fit the company's customer profile, he stormed into his boss's office and yelled, "I

Adapted from "How to Get Employees to Stop Worrying and Love AI," on hbr.org, January 25, 2018 (product #H044JQ).

don't want men and women over 55 buying our product! It's not our audience!" Maister demanded that the system vendor modify it to enable him to override its recommendations for how much to spend on each channel and for each audience target. The vendor scrambled to give him the controls he wanted. However, after being given the reins on budgeting and buying decisions, Maister saw his decisions were degrading results. For example, despite the company's younger customer profile, men and women over 55 were buying gifts for their children, nieces, and grandchildren, making them, in fact, a very profitable audience.

Maister returned control to the system and results improved. Over the ensuing weeks, he began to understand what the system did well, and what he could do to help it. He learned to leave decisions about where to spend and whom to target to the system. He focused on introducing more strategic parameters, such as the aggressiveness of a campaign or a limit on spending, and on testing different approaches to execution. The results continued to improve throughout the year as the system learned and got smarter, while Maister learned how to improve the brand's strategy in response to the insights produced by the AI. Within the first three months of using the system in new channels, the brand saw a 75% increase in purchases from paid digital channels, a 77% increase in purchase value, a 76% increase in return on ad spend, and a significant decrease in cost per acquisition.

The names in this story have been changed, but the moral is clear: If you give control over AI experiments to employees to keep them involved, and to allow them to see what the AI does well, you can leverage the best of both humans and machines.

Unfortunately, companies will be unable to take full advantage of the huge potential of AI if employees don't trust AI tools enough to turn their work over to them and let the machine run. This problem of low AI adoption rates is increasing as businesses of all kinds are seeing successful applications of AI and realizing it can be applied to many data-intensive processes and tasks even as AI technology—once only available to Tech Giants—is now becoming less expensive and easier for smaller companies to access and operate, thanks to AI-as-a-Service.

Resistance to disruptive, technology-driven change is not unusual. Specifically, many people resist AI because of the hype surrounding it, its lack of transparency, their fear of losing control over their work, and the way it disrupts familiar work patterns.

Consider these cases where humans interfered with an AI initiative, and the reasons behind them:

- **Loss of control.** A retailer implemented a website advertising optimization tool. The marketing team could upload a few different key banners or messages to the most prominent location on the website and, after gathering some experience, the system would decide which message produced the highest visitor engagement. It would then offer that up to future visitors. But the marketing team struggled with allowing the system to take control, and often intervened to show a message they preferred, undercutting the value of the tool.

- **Disruption of plans.** The CEO of a global lending institution was quickly sold on the financial benefits and operational efficiencies of introducing an AI-enabled system to take over lending decisions. But the vice president of analytics saw the new system as a diversion from his plans for his analytics teams and the company's technology investments. He scrambled to derail consideration of the new system. He described in detail what his analysts did and concluded, "There's no way this system is ever going to be able to produce the kinds of results they are claiming."

- **Disruption of relationships.** The head of e-commerce for a regional product group at a consumer products company stuck his neck out to get permission from global headquarters to run an experiment with an AI-enabled system on some of his product's ad campaigns. Initial tests demonstrated unprecedented results. In 2017, sales improved 15% due to the campaigns. But adoption beyond the regional group and the one product line stalled due to the resistance of people with long-standing, friendly relationships with the agencies that ran the company's ad campaigns, who would lose work to the machine.

So, what can companies do to help employees become more comfortable working with AI systems?

Being able to visualize the way an AI-enabled system arrives at its decisions helps develop trust in the system—opening the black box so people can see inside. For example, Albert, a provider of an AI-based tool that helps marketers make better advertising investment decisions and improves campaign performance, developed a visualization tool ("Inside Albert") for its users to see where and when their brand is performing best; what ad concepts are converting the most customers; who the ideal customer is in terms of gender, location, and social characteristics; and the total number of micro audience segments the system has created (often in the tens of thousands). Clients realized that they couldn't micromanage one set of variables, such as ad frequency, because the system was wading through and factoring in a vast number of variables to decide pace and timing. Though users initially felt like the system was not aware of what they believed to be their best performing days and frequency, they learned that the system was finding high conversions operating outside of their previously established assumptions. "Inside Albert" let marketers better understand how the system was making decisions, so they ultimately didn't feel the need to micromanage it.

To overcome the resistance of stakeholders who may not be willing to engage with the new system, such as the VP of analytics at the lending institution, another approach is to build political momentum for a new AI-enabled system by mobilizing stakeholders who benefit from its adoption. For example, Waymo has partnered with Mothers Against Drunk Driving, the National Safety Council, the Foundation for Blind Children, and the Foundation for Senior Living to rally these constituencies in support of self-driving cars.

As AI is increasingly deployed throughout your company's decision-making processes, the goal should be to transition as quickly as possible. As the examples of Albert and Waymo illustrate, you can overcome AI resistance by running experiments, creating a way to visualize the decision process of the AI, and engaging constituencies who would benefit from the technology. The sooner you get people on board, the sooner your company will be able to see the potential results that AI can produce.

Brad Power is the founder of CancerHacker Lab.

CHAPTER 13

A Better Way to Onboard AI

by Boris Babic, Daniel L. Chen, Theodoros Evgeniou, and Anne-Laure Fayard

In a 2018 Workforce Institute survey of 3,000 managers across eight industrialized nations, the majority of respondents described artificial intelligence as a valuable productivity tool.

It's easy to see why: AI brings tangible benefits in processing speed, accuracy, and consistency, which is why many professionals now rely on it. Some medical specialists, for example, use AI tools to help make diagnoses and decisions about treatment.

But respondents to that survey also expressed fears that AI would take their jobs. They are not alone. The

---

Adapted from an article in *Harvard Business Review*, July–August 2020 (product #R4004C).

Guardian recently reported that more than 6 million workers in the United Kingdom fear being replaced by machines. These fears are echoed by academics and executives we meet at conferences and seminars. AI's advantages can be cast in a much darker light: Why would humans be needed when machines can do a better job?

The prevalence of such fears suggests that organizations looking to reap the benefits of AI need to be careful when introducing it to the people expected to work with it. Andrew Wilson, until January 2020 Accenture's CIO, says, "The greater the degree of organizational focus on people helping AI, and AI helping people, the greater the value achieved." Accenture has found that when companies make it clear that they are using AI to help people rather than to replace them, they significantly outperform companies that don't set that objective (or are unclear about their AI goals) along most dimensions of managerial productivity—notably speed, scalability, and effectiveness of decision-making.

In other words, just as when new talent joins a team, AI must be set up to succeed rather than to fail. A smart employer trains new hires by giving them simple tasks that build hands-on experience in a noncritical context and assigns them mentors to offer help and advice. This allows the newcomers to learn while others focus on higher-value tasks. As they gain experience and demonstrate that they can do the job, their mentors increasingly rely on them as sounding boards and entrust them

---

Disclosure: Theodoros Evgeniou is an adviser to Marble Bar Asset Management (an investment firm named in this article).

with more-substantive decisions. Over time an apprentice becomes a partner, contributing skills and insight.

We believe this approach can work for artificial intelligence as well. In the following pages we draw on our own and others' research and consulting on AI and information systems implementation, along with organizational studies of innovation and work practices, to present a four-phase approach to implementing AI. It allows enterprises to cultivate people's trust—a key condition for adoption—and to work toward a distributed human-AI cognitive system in which people and AI *both* continually improve. Many organizations have experimented with phase 1, and some have progressed to phases 2 and 3. For now, phase 4 may be mostly a "future-casting" exercise of which we see some early signs, but it is feasible from a technological perspective and would provide more value to companies as they engage with artificial intelligence.

Phase 1: The Assistant

This first phase of onboarding artificial intelligence is rather like the process of training an assistant. You teach the new employee a few fundamental rules and hand over some basic but time-consuming tasks you normally do (such as filing online forms or summarizing documents), which frees you to focus on more-important aspects of the job. The trainee learns by watching you, performing the tasks, and asking questions.

One common task for AI assistants is sorting data. An example is the recommendation systems companies have used since the mid-1990s to help customers filter thousands of products and find the ones most relevant to them—Amazon and Netflix being among the leaders in this technology.

More and more business decisions now require this type of data sorting. When, for example, portfolio managers are choosing stocks in which to invest, the information available is far more than a human can feasibly process, and new information comes out all the time, adding to the historical record. Software can make the task more manageable by immediately filtering stocks to meet predefined investment criteria. Natural-language processing, meanwhile, can identify the news most relevant to a company and even assess the general sentiment about an upcoming corporate event as reflected in analysts' reports. Marble Bar Asset Management (MBAM), a London-based investment firm founded in 2002, is an early convert to using such technologies in the workplace. It has developed a state-of-the-art platform, called RAID (Research Analysis and Information Database), to help portfolio managers filter through high volumes of information about corporate events, news developments, and stock movements.

Another way AI can lend assistance is to model what a human might do. As anyone who uses Google will have noticed, prompts appear as a search phrase is typed in. Predictive text on a smartphone offers a similar way to speed up the process of typing. This kind of user modeling, related to what is sometimes called *judgmental bootstrapping,* was developed more than 30 years ago; it can easily be applied to decision-making. AI would use it to identify the choice an employee is most likely to make, given that employee's past choices, and would suggest that choice as a starting point when the employee is faced with multiple decisions—speeding up, rather than actually doing, the job.

Let's look at this in a specific context. When airline employees are deciding how much food and drink to put on a given flight, they fill out catering orders, which involve a certain amount of calculation together with assumptions based on their experience of previous flights. Making the wrong choices incurs costs: Underordering risks upsetting customers who may avoid future travel on the airline. Overordering means the excess food will go to waste and the plane will have increased its fuel consumption unnecessarily.

An algorithm can be very helpful in this context. AI can predict what the airline's catering manager would order by analyzing their past choices or using rules set by the manager. This "autocomplete" of "recommended orders" can be customized for every flight using all relevant historical data, including food and drink consumption on the route in question and even past purchasing behavior by passengers on the manifest for that flight. But as with predictive typing, human users can freely overwrite as needed; they are always in the driver's seat. AI simply assists them by imitating or anticipating their decision style.

It should not be a stretch for managers to work with AI in this way. We already do so in our personal lives, when we allow the autocomplete function to prefill forms for us online. In the workplace a manager can, for example, define specific rules for an AI assistant to follow when completing forms. In fact, many software tools currently used in the workplace (such as credit-rating programs) are already just that: collections of human-defined decision rules. The AI assistant can refine the rules by codifying the circumstances under which the manager actually follows them. This learning needn't involve any change in the manager's behavior, let alone any effort to "teach" the assistant.

Phase 2: The Monitor

The next step is to set up the AI system to provide real-time feedback. Thanks to machine learning programs, AI can be trained to accurately forecast what a user's decision would be in a given situation (absent lapses in rationality owing to, for example, overconfidence or fatigue). If a user is about to make a choice that is inconsistent with their choice history, the system can flag the discrepancy. This is especially helpful during high-volume decision-making, when human employees may be tired or distracted.

Research in psychology, behavioral economics, and cognitive science shows that humans have limited and imperfect reasoning capabilities, especially when it comes to statistical and probabilistic problems, which are ubiquitous in business. Several studies (of which one of us, Chen, is a coauthor) concerning legal decisions found that judges grant political asylum more frequently before lunch than after, that they give lighter prison sentences if their NFL team won the previous day than if it lost, and that they will go easier on a defendant on the latter's birthday. Clearly justice might be better served if human decision-makers were assisted by software that told them when a decision they were planning to make was inconsistent with their prior decisions or with the decision that an analysis of purely legal variables would predict.

AI can deliver that kind of input. Another study (also with Chen as a coauthor) showed that AI programs processing a model made up of basic legal variables (constructed by the study's authors) can predict asylum decisions with roughly 80% accuracy on the date a case opens. The authors have added learning functionality to the program, which enables it to simulate the decision-making of an individual judge by drawing on that judge's past decisions.

The approach translates well to other contexts. For example, when portfolio managers (PMs) at Marble Bar Asset Management consider buy or sell decisions that may raise the overall portfolio risk—for example, by increasing exposure to a particular sector or geography—the system alerts them through a pop-up during a computerized transaction process so that they can adjust appropriately. A PM may ignore such feedback as long as company risk limits are observed. But in any case, the feedback helps the PM reflect on their decisions.

Of course AI is not always "right." Often its suggestions don't take into account some reliable private information to which the human decision-maker has access, so the AI might steer an employee off course rather than simply correct for possible behavioral biases. That's why using it should be like a dialogue, in which the algorithm provides nudges according to the data it has while the human teaches the AI by explaining why they overrode a particular nudge. This improves the AI's usefulness and preserves the autonomy of the human decision-maker.

Unfortunately, many AI systems are set up to usurp that autonomy. Once an algorithm has flagged a bank transaction as possibly fraudulent, for example, employees are often unable to approve the transaction without clearing it with a supervisor or even an outside auditor. Sometimes undoing a machine's choice is next to impossible—a persistent source of frustration for both customers and customer service professionals. In many cases the rationale for an AI choice is opaque, and employees are in no position to question that choice even when mistakes have been made.

Privacy is another big issue when machines collect data on the decisions people make. In addition to giving humans control in their exchanges with AI, we need to guarantee that any data it collects on them is kept confidential. A wall ought to separate the engineering team from management; otherwise, employees may worry that if they freely interact with the system and make mistakes, they might later suffer for them.

Also, companies should set rules about designing and interacting with AI to ensure organizational consistency in norms and practices. These rules might specify the level of predictive accuracy required to show a nudge or to offer a reason for one; criteria for the necessity of a nudge; and the conditions under which an employee should either follow the AI's instruction or refer it to a superior rather than accept or reject it.

To help employees retain their sense of control in phase 2, we advise managers and systems designers to involve them in design: Engage them as experts to define the data that will be used and to determine ground truth; familiarize them with models during development; and provide training and interaction as those models are deployed. In the process, employees will see how the models are built, how the data is managed, and why the machines make the recommendations they do.

Phase 3: The Coach

In a recent PwC survey nearly 60% of respondents said that they would like to get performance feedback on a daily or a weekly basis. It's not hard to see why. As Peter Drucker asserted in his famous *Harvard Business Review* article "Managing Oneself," people generally don't know what they are good at. And when they think they do know, they are usually wrong.

The trouble is that the only way to discover strengths and opportunities for improvement is through a careful analysis of key decisions and actions. That requires documenting expectations about outcomes and then, nine months to a year later, comparing those expectations with what actually happened. Thus the feedback employees get usually comes from hierarchical superiors during a review—not at a time or in a format of the recipient's choosing. That is unfortunate, because, as Tessa West of New York University found in a recent neuroscience study, the more people feel that their autonomy is protected and that they are in control of the conversation—

able to choose, for example, when feedback is given—the better they respond to it.

AI could address this problem. The capabilities we've already mentioned could easily generate feedback for employees, enabling them to look at their own performance and reflect on variations and errors. A monthly summary analyzing data drawn from their past behavior might help them better understand their decision patterns and practices. A few companies, notably in the financial sector, are taking this approach. Portfolio managers at MBAM, for example, receive feedback from a data analytics system that captures investment decisions at the individual level.

The data can reveal interesting and varying biases among PMs. Some may be more loss-averse than others, holding on to underperforming investments longer than they should. Others may be overconfident, possibly taking on too large a position in a given investment. The analysis identifies these behaviors and—like a coach—provides personalized feedback that highlights behavioral changes over time, suggesting how to improve decisions. But it is up to the PMs to decide how to incorporate the feedback. MBAM's leadership believes this "trading enhancement" is becoming a core differentiator that both helps develop portfolio managers and makes the organization more attractive.

What's more, just as a good mentor learns from the insights of the people who are being mentored, a machine learning "coachbot" learns from the decisions of an empowered human employee. In the relationship we've described, a human can disagree with the coachbot—and that creates new data that will change the AI's implicit model. For example, if a portfolio manager decides not to trade a highlighted stock because of recent company events, they can provide an explanation to the system. With feedback, the system continually captures data that can be analyzed to provide insights.

If employees can relate to and control exchanges with artificial intelligence, they are more likely to see it as a safe channel for feedback that aims to help rather than to assess performance. Choosing the right interface is useful to this end. At MBAM, for example, trading enhancement tools—visuals, for instance—are personalized to reflect a PM's preferences.

As in phase 2, involving employees in designing the system is essential. When AI is a coach, people will be even more fearful of disempowerment. It can easily seem like a competitor as well as a partner—and who wants to feel less intelligent than a machine? Concerns about autonomy and privacy may be even stronger. Working with a coach requires honesty, and people may hesitate to be open with one that might share unflattering data with the folks in HR.

Deploying AI in the ways described in the first three phases does of course have some downsides. Over the long term, new technologies create more jobs than they destroy, but meanwhile labor markets may be painfully disrupted. What's more, as Matt Beane argues in "Learning to Work with Intelligent Machines" (HBR, September–October 2019), companies that deploy AI can leave employees with fewer opportunities for hands-on learning and mentorship. There is some risk, therefore, not only of losing entry-level jobs (because digital assistants can effectively replace human ones) but also of compromising the ability of future decision-makers to think for themselves. That's not inevitable, however. As Beane suggests, companies could use their artificial intelligence to create different and better learning opportunities for their employees while improving the system by making it more transparent and giving employees more control. Because future entrants to the workforce will have grown up in a human-plus-machine workplace, they will almost certainly be faster than their pre-AI colleagues at spotting opportunities to innovate and introduce activities that add value and create jobs—which brings us to the final phase.

Phase 4: The Teammate

Edwin Hutchins, a cognitive anthropologist, developed what is known as the theory of distributed cognition. It is based on his study of ship navigation, which, he showed, involved a combination of sailors, charts, rulers, compasses, and a plotting tool. The theory broadly relates to the concept of extended mind, which posits that cognitive processing, and associated mental acts such as belief and intention, are not necessarily limited to the brain, or even the body. External tools and instruments can, under the right conditions, play a role in cognitive processing and create what is known as a *coupled system*.

In line with this thinking, in the final phase of the AI implementation journey (which to our knowledge no organization has yet adopted) companies would develop a coupled network of humans and machines in which both contribute expertise. We believe that as AI improves through its interactions with individual users, analyzing and even modeling expert users by drawing on data about their past decisions and behaviors, a community of experts (humans and machines) will naturally emerge in organizations that have fully integrated AI coachbots. For example, a purchasing manager who—with one click at the moment of decision—could see what price someone else would give could benefit from a customized collective of experts.

Although the technology to create this kind of collective intelligence now exists, this phase is fraught with challenges. For example, any such integration of AI must avoid building in old or new biases and must respect human privacy concerns so that people can trust the AI as much as they would a human partner. That in itself is a pretty big challenge, given the volume of research demonstrating how hard it is to build trust among humans.

The best approaches to building trust in the workplace rely on the relationship between trust and understanding—a subject of study by David Danks and colleagues at Carnegie Mellon. According to this model, I trust someone because I understand that person's values, desires, and intentions, and they demonstrate that they have my best interests at heart. Although understanding has historically been a basis for building trust in human relationships, it is potentially well suited to cultivating human–AI partnerships as well, because employees' fear of artificial intelligence is usually grounded in a lack of understanding of how AI works.

In building understanding, a particular challenge is defining what "explanation" means—let alone "good explanation." This challenge is the focus of a lot of research. For example, one of us (Evgeniou) is working to open up machine learning "black boxes" by means of so-called counterfactual explanations. A counterfactual explanation illuminates a particular decision of an AI system (for example, to approve credit for a given transaction) by identifying a short list of transaction characteristics that drove the decision one way or another. Had any of the characteristics been different (or counter to the fact), the system would have made a different decision (credit would have been denied).

Evgeniou is also exploring what people perceive as good explanations for AI decisions. For example, do they see an explanation as better when it's presented in terms of a logical combination of features ("The transaction was approved because it had XYZ characteristics") or when it's presented relative to other decisions ("The transaction was approved because it looks like other approved transactions, and here they are for you to see")? As research into what makes AI explainable continues, AI systems should become more transparent, thus facilitating trust.

Conclusion

Adopting new technologies has always been a major challenge—and the more impact a technology has, the bigger the challenge is. Because of its potential impact, artificial intelligence may be perceived as particularly difficult to implement. Yet if done mindfully, adoption can be fairly smooth. That is precisely why companies must ensure that AI's design and development are responsible—especially with regard to transparency, decision autonomy, and privacy—and that it engages the people who will be working with it. Otherwise they will quite reasonably fear being constrained—or even replaced—by machines that are making all sorts of decisions in ways they don't understand.

Getting past these fears to create a trusting relationship with AI is key. In all four phases described in these pages, humans determine the ground rules. With a responsible design, AI may become a true partner in the workplace—rapidly processing large volumes of varied data in a consistent manner to enhance the intuition and creativity of humans, who in turn teach the machine.

Boris Babic is an assistant professor of decision sciences at INSEAD. **Daniel L. Chen** is a professor at the Institute for Advanced Study at the Toulouse School of Economics and lead investigator at the World Bank's Data and Evidence for Justice Reform program. **Theodoros Evgeniou** is a professor at INSEAD. **Anne-Laure Fayard** is an associate professor of innovation, design, and organization studies at NYU's Tandon School of Engineering.

CHAPTER 14

Managing AI Decision-Making Tools

by Michael Ross and James Taylor

Your business's use of AI is only going to increase, and that's a good thing. Digitalization allows businesses to operate at an atomic level and make millions of decisions each day about a single customer, product, supplier, asset, or transaction. But these decisions cannot be made by humans working in a spreadsheet.

We call these granular, AI-powered decisions "microdecisions" (borrowed from Taylor and Raden's book *Smart Enough Systems*). They require a complete

---

Adapted from content posted on hbr.org, November 10, 2021 (product #H06ORA).

paradigm shift, a move from making decisions to making "decisions about decisions." You must manage at a new level of abstraction through rules, parameters, and algorithms. This shift is happening across every industry and across all kinds of decision-making. In this article we propose a framework for how to think about these decisions and how to determine the optimal management model.

Micro-Decisions Require Automation

The nature of micro-decisions requires some level of automation, particularly for real-time and higher-volume decisions. Automation is enabled by algorithms (the rules, predictions, constraints, and logic that determine how a micro-decision is made). And these decision-making algorithms are often described as AI. The critical question is, how do human managers manage these types of algorithm-powered systems?

An autonomous system is conceptually very easy. Imagine a driverless car without a steering wheel. The driver simply tells the car where to go and hopes for the best. But the moment there's a steering wheel, you have a problem. You must inform the driver when they might want to intervene, how they can intervene, and how much notice you will give them when the need to intervene arises. You must think carefully about the information you will present to the driver to help them make an appropriate intervention.

The same is true for any micro-decision. The moment there is a human involved, you need to think carefully about how to design a decision system that enables the human to have a meaningful interaction with the machine.

The four main management models we developed vary based on the level and nature of the human intervention: We call them "human in the loop (HITL), "human in the loop for exceptions" (HITLFE), "human on the loop" (HOTL), and "human out of the loop" (HOOTL). It's important to recognize this is a spectrum, and while we have pulled out the key management models, there are subvariants based on the split between human and machine, and the level of management abstraction at which the human engages with the system.

The Range of Management Options

Human in the loop (HITL)

A human is assisted by a machine. In this model, the human is doing the decision-making and the machine is providing only decision support or partial automation of all or part of some decisions. This is often referred to as intelligence amplification.

Collecting and disposing of waste and recycling is a complex business where everything from the weather to local noise ordinances, parking lot layouts to gate locks, recycling types to dump locations, driver availability, and truck capabilities all play a role in an efficient operation. A *Fortune* 500 company is investing heavily in using AI to improve its operations. It recognizes that the value of AI often comes from helping humans do their job better. One example is in helping the dispatchers handle tickets and routes more effectively. Many things can prevent a smooth service event: for example, the need for a specific key or code, time windows when pickup is or is not possible, width and length restrictions, instructions for getting things moved or opened, temporary construction, and much more.

A recently developed bot crawls through all the tickets and requests in multiple systems to identify anything that might impact a particular stop and brings it to the dispatcher's attention. It proactively identifies all the possible issues for the route as currently set up (and redoes this when stops are added, moved, or removed during the day) and can be used reactively by dispatchers as they work to find the best way to add requests to in-flight routes. The human dispatcher monitors the system as it works to free up 20% to 25% of their day by automating thousands of decisions about service tickets.

Human in the loop for exceptions (HITLFE)

Most decisions are automated in this model, and the human only handles exceptions. The exceptions occur when the system requires some judgment or input from the human before it can make the decision, though it is unlikely to ask the human to make the whole decision. Humans also control the logic to determine which exceptions are flagged for review.

A beauty brand developed a machine learning (ML) algorithm to predict the sales uplift for different types of promotion to replace an existing human-powered approach. The ML prediction took account of such factors as the offer, marketing support, seasonality, and cannibalization to create an automated forecast. For many promotions, the ML prediction worked well, but managers lost confidence after initial success was quickly followed by some extreme failures, which resulted in significant lost sales. When the data scientists reviewed the predictions, they found that the ML algorithm struggled to predict certain types of promotion. Rather than abandoning the project, they developed a HITLFE approach. The key was to codify the machine's level of confidence in its predictions and have the humans review predictions on an exception basis when the machine had low confidence.

Human on the loop (HOTL)

Here, the machine is assisted by a human. The machine makes the micro-decisions, but the human reviews the decision outcomes and can adjust rules and parameters for future decisions. In a more advanced setup, the machine also recommends parameters or rule changes that are then approved by a human.

A European food delivery business needed to manage its fleet of cyclists and used a spreadsheet to plan the number of "delivery slots" required over the next hour/day/week. It then deployed various incentives: for example, increasing the per delivery rate to match driver supply with expected demand. This was a highly manual and imprecise process, and the company decided to develop a completely automated system to test against its manual approach. The results were interesting. Sometimes the humans performed better; sometimes the machine performed better. The company realized that it had framed the problem incorrectly. The real question was how to get the humans and machines to collaborate. This led to a second approach in which, rather than the humans managing at the driver level, the company designed a set of control parameters that allowed the managers to make a trade-off of risk, cost, and service. This approach acknowledged the dynamic nature of the system, the need to make trade-offs that might change over time, and the critical need to keep the jobs interesting!

Human out of the loop (HOOTL)

In this model, the machine is monitored by the human. The machine makes every decision, and the human intervenes only by setting new constraints and objectives. Improvement is also an automated closed loop. Adjustments, based on feedback from humans, are automated.

The *Mayflower Autonomous Ship* is exploring the world's ocean using radar, GPS, AI-powered cameras, dozens of sensors, and multiple edge computing devices. But it does not have a crew. With humans completely out of the loop, the *Mayflower* must sense its environment, predict courses, identify hazards, apply collision regulations, and obey the rules of the sea. Its AI captain does this autonomously, moving to achieve the goals set in advance by the humans in charge of the project. The humans, back onshore, simply tell it where to go.

Deciding Which Model Is Right for You

It's important to recognize that these systems will evolve over time, enabled by new technology, an organizations' desire to make ever more surgical decisions, and greater management confidence in automation. You must decide what level of human management is possible and desirable, and your appetite for risk and iteration. There is no correct answer.

Whichever model you adopt, we believe it's critical to put the AI on the org chart and in the process design to ensure that human managers feel responsible for its output. The need for more autonomous systems, consumer demand for instant responses, real-time coordination of supply chains, and remote, automated environments are all combining to make increased AI use within your organization an inevitability. These systems will be making increasingly fine-grained micro-decisions on your behalf, impacting your customers, your employees, your partners, and your suppliers. To succeed, you need to understand the different ways you can interact with AI and pick the right management option for each of your AI systems.

Michael Ross is a cofounder of DynamicAction, which provides cloud-based data analytics to retail companies, and an executive fellow at London Business School. **James Taylor** is the founder and CEO of Decision Management Solutions. He's an expert in how to use decision modeling, business rules, and analytic technology for digital decision-making. He's the author of several books, including *Digital Decisioning: Using Decision Management to Deliver Business Impact from AI*.

CHAPTER 15

Your Company's Algorithms Will Go Wrong. Have a Plan in Place.

by Roman V. Yampolskiy

When you're ready to incorporate artificial intelligence technologies in your business, the analysis you should perform is this: What can possibly go wrong? What is our product or service expected to do? What happens if it fails to do so? Do we have a damage mitigation plan? Consider the embarrassing situation that Microsoft found itself in with its Tay chatbot fiasco, where internet trolls exploited vulnerabilities in the bot's code, feeding

---

Adapted from "What Will Happen When Your Company's Algorithms Go Wrong?" on hbr.org, April 10, 2017 (product #H03L3S).

it racist, homophobic, and sexist content that millions read on social media.

Accidents, including deadly ones, caused by software or industrial robots can be traced to the early days of such technology, but they are not necessarily caused by the systems themselves. AI failures, on the other hand, are directly related to the mistakes produced by the intelligence such systems are designed to exhibit. We can broadly classify such failures into "mistakes made during the learning phase" and "mistakes made during performance phase." A system can fail to learn what its designers want it to learn and might instead learn a different, but correlated function.

A frequently cited example is a computer vision system that the U.S. Army had hoped to use to automatically detect camouflaged enemy tanks. The system was supposed to classify pictures of tanks, but instead learned to distinguish the backgrounds of such images. Other examples include problems caused by poorly designed functions that would reward AIs for only partially desirable behaviors, such as pausing a game to avoid losing, or repeatedly touching a soccer ball to get credit for possession.

It can help to look at some recent examples of AI failure to better understand what problems are likely to arise and what you can do to prevent them—or at least to clean up quickly after a failure. Consider these real examples of AI failures:

- An automated email reply generator created inappropriate responses, such as writing "I love you" to a business colleague.

- A robot for grabbing auto parts grabbed and killed a man.

- Image-tagging software classified Black people as gorillas.

- Medical AI classified patients with asthma as having a lower risk of dying of pneumonia.

- Adult-content-filtering software failed to remove inappropriate content, exposing children to violent and sexual content.

- AI designed to predict recidivism acted racist.

- An AI agent exploited a reward signal to win a game without actually completing the game.

- Video game NPCs (non-player characters, or any character that is not controlled by a human player) designed unauthorized superweapons.

- AI judged a beauty contest and rated dark-skinned contestants lower.

- A mall security robot collided with and injured a child.

- The AI "AlphaGo" lost to a human in a world-championship-level game of "Go."

- A self-driving car had a deadly accident.

And every day, consumers experience more common shortcomings of AI: Spam filters block important emails, GPS provides faulty directions, machine translations corrupt the meaning of phrases, autocorrect replaces a desired word with a wrong one, biometric systems misrecognize people, transcription software fails to capture what is being said; overall, it is harder to find examples of AIs that *don't* fail.

Analyzing the list of AI failures above, we can arrive at a simple generalization: An AI designed to do X will eventually fail to do X. While it may seem trivial, it is a powerful generalization tool, which can be used to predict future failures of AIs. For example, looking at cutting-edge current and future AIs we can predict that:

- AI doctors will misdiagnose some patients in a way a real doctor would not.

- Video description software will misunderstand movie plots.

- Software for generating jokes will occasionally fail to make them funny.

- Sarcasm detection software will confuse sarcastic and sincere statements.

- Employee-screening software will be systematically biased and thus hire low performers.

- A Mars robot-explorer will misjudge its environment and fall into a crater.

- Tax preparation software will miss important deductions or make inappropriate ones.

What should you learn from the above examples and analysis? Failures will happen! It's inevitable. But we can still put best practices in place, such as:

- Controlling user input to the system and limiting learning to verified data inputs

- Checking for racial, gender, age, and other common biases in your algorithms

- Explicitly analyzing how your software can fail and then providing a safety mechanism for each possible failure

- Having a less "smart" backup product or service available

- Having a communications plan in place to address the media in case of an embarrassing failure (hint: start with an apology)

I predict that both the frequency and seriousness of AI failures will steadily increase as AIs become more capable. The failures of today's narrow-domain AIs are just the tip of the iceberg; once we develop general artificial intelligence capable of cross-domain performance, embarrassment will be the least of our concerns.

Roman V. Yampolskiy is a tenured associate professor in the department of computer engineering and computer science at the Speed School of Engineering, University of Louisville. He is the founding and current director of the university's cybersecurity lab and an author of many books, including *Artificial Superintelligence: A Futuristic Approach*. Follow him on Twitter @romanyam.

SECTION FIVE

Managing Ethics and Bias

CHAPTER 16

A Practical Guide to Ethical AI

by Reid Blackman

Companies are leveraging data and artificial intelligence to create scalable solutions—but they're also scaling their reputational, regulatory, and legal risks. For instance, in 2019 alone, Los Angeles sued IBM for allegedly misappropriating data it collected with its ubiquitous weather app; Optum was investigated by regulators for creating an algorithm that allegedly recommended that doctors and nurses pay more attention to white patients than to sicker Black patients; and Goldman Sachs was investigated by regulators for using an AI algorithm that allegedly discriminated against women by granting

---

Adapted from content posted on hbr.org, October 15, 2020 (reprint #H05XNT).

larger credit limits to men than women on their Apple cards. Ultimately, IBM settled out of court, and Optum pledged to remove race from certain diagnostic algorithms. Goldman Sachs was cleared of wrongdoing but was still widely scolded for its responses to concerned customers.

These examples indicate how discussions of "data ethics" and "AI ethics" are now everyone's concern. A few years ago, these terms were reserved for nonprofit organizations and academics. Today the biggest tech companies in the world are putting together fast-growing teams to tackle the ethical problems that arise from the widespread collection, analysis, and use of massive troves of data, particularly when that data is used to train machine learning models, aka AI.

These companies are investing in answers to once esoteric ethical questions because they've realized one simple truth: Failing to operationalize data and AI ethics is a threat to the bottom line. Missing the mark can expose companies to reputational, regulatory, and legal risks, but that's not the half of it. Failing to operationalize data and AI ethics leads to wasted resources, inefficiencies in product development and deployment, and even an inability to use data to train AI models at all. For example, Amazon engineers reportedly spent years working on AI hiring software but eventually scrapped the program because they couldn't figure out how to create a model that doesn't systematically discriminate against women. Sidewalk Labs, a subsidiary of Google, faced massive backlash by citizens and local government officials over their plans to build an internet-of-things–fueled "smart city" within Toronto due to a lack of clear ethical standards for the project's data handling. The company ultimately scrapped the project at a loss of two years of work and USD $50 million.

Despite the costs of getting it wrong, most companies grapple with data and AI ethics through ad hoc discussions on a per-product basis. With no clear protocol in place on how to identify, evaluate, and mitigate the risks, teams end up either overlooking risks, scrambling to solve issues as they come up, or crossing their fingers in the hope that the problem will resolve itself. When companies have attempted to tackle the issue at scale, they've tended to implement strict, imprecise, and overly broad policies that lead to false positives in risk identification and stymied production. These problems grow by orders of magnitude when you introduce third-party vendors, who may or may not be thinking about these questions at all.

Companies need a plan for mitigating risk—how to use data and develop AI products without falling into ethical pitfalls along the way. Just like other risk-management strategies, an operationalized approach to data and AI ethics must systematically and exhaustively identify ethical risks throughout the organization, from IT to HR to marketing to product and beyond.

What Not to Do

Putting the larger tech companies to the side, there are three standard approaches to data and AI ethical risk mitigation, none of which bear fruit.

First, there is the *academic approach*. Academics—and I speak from 15 years of experience as a former professor of philosophy—are fantastic at rigorous and systematic inquiry. Those academics who are ethicists (typically found in philosophy departments) are adept at spotting ethical problems, their sources, and how to think through them. But while academic ethicists might seem like a perfect match, given the need for systematic identification and mitigation of ethical risks, they unfortunately tend to ask different questions than businesses. For the most part, academics ask, "Should we do this? Would it be good for society overall? Does it conduce to human flourishing?" Businesses, on the other hand, tend to ask, "Given that we are going to do this, how can we do it without making ourselves vulnerable to ethical risks?"

The result is academic treatments that do not speak to the highly particular, concrete uses of data and AI. This translates to the absence of clear directives to the developers on the ground and the senior leaders who need to identify and choose among a set of risk-mitigation strategies.

Next, is the *"on-the-ground" approach*. Within businesses those asking the questions are standardly enthusiastic engineers, data scientists, and product managers. They know to ask the business-relevant, risk-related questions precisely because they are the ones making the products to achieve particular business goals. What they lack, however, is the kind of training that academics receive. As a result, they do not have the skill, knowledge, and experience to answer ethical questions systematically, exhaustively, and efficiently. They also lack a critical ingredient: institutional support.

Finally, there are companies (not to mention countries) rolling out *high-level AI ethics principles*. Google and Microsoft, for instance, trumpeted their principles years ago. The difficulty comes in operationalizing those principles. What, exactly, does it mean to be for "fairness"? What are engineers to do when confronted with the dozens of definitions and accompanying metrics for fairness in the computer science literature? Which metric is the right one in any given case, and who makes that judgment? For most companies—including those tech companies who are actively trying to solve the problem—there are no clear answers to these questions. Indeed, seeming coalescence around a shared set of abstract values actually obscures widespread misalignment.

How to Operationalize Data and AI Ethics

AI ethics does not come in a box. Given the varying values of companies across dozens of industries, a data and AI ethics program must be tailored to the specific business and regulatory needs that are relevant to the company. However, here are seven steps toward building a customized, operationalized, scalable, and sustainable data and AI ethics program.

1. Identify existing infrastructure that a data and AI ethics program can leverage

The key to a successful creation of a data and AI ethics program is using the power and authority of existing infrastructure, such as a data governance board that convenes to discuss privacy, cyber, compliance, and other data-related risks. This allows concerns from those "on the ground" (e.g., product owners and managers) to bubble up and, when necessary, they can in turn elevate key concerns to relevant executives. Governance board buy-in works for a few reasons: (1) The executive level sets the tone for how seriously employees will take these issues, (2) a data and AI ethics strategy needs to dovetail with the general data and AI strategy, which is devised at the executive level, and (3) protecting the brand from reputational, regulatory, and legal risk is ultimately a C-suite responsibility, and those people need to be alerted when high-stakes issues arise.

If such a body does not exist then companies can create one—an ethics council or committee, for example—with ethics-adjacent personnel, such as those in cyber, risk and compliance, privacy, and analytics. It may also be advisable to include external subject matter experts, including ethicists.

2. Create a data and AI ethical risk framework that is tailored to your industry

A good framework comprises, at a minimum, an articulation of the ethical standards—including the ethical nightmares—of the company, an identification of the relevant external and internal stakeholders, a recommended governance structure, and an articulation of how that structure will be maintained in the face of changing personnel and circumstances. It is important to establish KPIs and a quality assurance program to measure the continued effectiveness of the tactics carrying out your strategy.

A robust framework also makes clear how ethical risk mitigation is built into operations. For instance, it should identify the ethical standards data collectors, product developers, and product managers and owners must adhere to. It should also articulate a clear process by which ethical concerns are elevated to more senior leadership or to an ethics committee. All companies should ask whether there are processes in place that vet for biased algorithms, privacy violations, and unexplainable outputs.

Still, frameworks also need to be tailored to a company's industry. In finance, it is important to think about how digital identities are determined and how international transactions can be ethically safe. In health care there will need to be extra protections built around privacy, particularly as AI enables the development of precision medicine. In the retail space, where recommendation engines loom large, it is important to develop methods to detect and mitigate associative bias, in which recommendations flow from stereotypical and sometimes offensive associations with various populations.

3. Change how you think about ethics by taking cues from the successes in health care

Many senior leaders describe ethics in general—and data and AI ethics in particular—as "squishy" or "fuzzy," and argue it is not sufficiently "concrete" to be actionable. Leaders should take inspiration from health care, an industry that has been systematically focused on ethical risk mitigation since at least the 1970s. Key concerns about what constitutes privacy, self-determination, and informed consent, for example, have been explored deeply by medical ethicists, health care practitioners, regulators, and lawyers. Those insights can be transferred to many ethical dilemmas around consumer data privacy and control.

For instance, companies claim to respect the users of their products, but what does that mean in practice? In health care, an essential tenet of respect for patients is that they are treated only after they have granted informed consent—understood to include consent that, at a minimum, does not result from lies, manipulation, or communication in language the patient cannot understand, such as impenetrable legalese or Latin medical terms. These same requirements can be brought to bear on how people's data is collected, used, and shared. Ensuring that users are not only informed of how their data is being used but also that they are informed early on and in a way that makes comprehension likely (for instance, by not burying the information in a long legal document) is one easy lesson to take from health care. The more general lesson is to break down big ethical concepts like privacy, bias, and explainability into infrastructure, process, and practice that realize those values.

4. Optimize guidance and tools for product managers

While your framework provides high-level guidance, it's essential that guidance at the product level is granular. Take, for instance, the oft-lauded value of explainability in AI, a highly valued feature of ML models that will likely be part of your framework. Standard machine learning algorithms engage in pattern recognition too unwieldy for humans to grasp. But it is common—particularly when the outputs of the AI are potentially life-altering—to want or demand explanations for AI outputs. The problem is that there is often a tension between making outputs explainable, on the one hand, and making the outputs (e.g., predictions) accurate, on the other.

Product managers need to know how to make that tradeoff, and customized tools should be developed to help product managers make those decisions. For example, companies can create a tool by which project managers can evaluate the importance of explainability for a given product. If explainability is desirable because it helps to ferret out bias in an algorithm, but biased outputs are not a concern for this particular ML application, then that downgrades the importance of explainability relative to accuracy. If the outputs are subject to regulations that require explanations—for instance, regulations in the banking industry that require banks to explain why someone has been turned down for a loan—then explainability will be imperative. The same goes for other relevant values, e.g., which, if any, of the dozens of metrics to use when determining whether a product delivers fair or equitable outputs.

5. Build organizational awareness

Ten years ago, corporations scarcely paid attention to cyber risks, but they certainly do now, and employees are expected to have a grasp of some of those risks. Anyone who touches data or AI products—be they in HR, marketing, or operations—should understand the company's data and AI ethics framework. Creating a culture in which a data and AI ethics strategy can be successfully deployed and maintained requires educating and upskilling employees and empowering them to raise important questions at crucial junctures and bring key concerns to the appropriate deliberative body. Throughout this process, it's important to clearly articulate why data and AI ethics matter to the organization in a way that demonstrates the commitment is not merely part of a public relations campaign.

6. Formally and informally incentivize employees to play a role in identifying AI ethical risks

We know that ethical standards are compromised when people are financially incentivized to act unethically. Similarly, failing to financially incentivize ethical actions can lead to them being deprioritized. A company's values are partly determined by how it directs financial resources. When employees don't see a budget behind scaling and maintaining a strong data and AI ethics program, they will turn their attention to what moves them forward in their career. Rewarding people for their efforts in promoting a data ethics program is essential.

7. Monitor impacts and engage stakeholders

Creating organizational awareness, ethics committees, and informed product managers, engineers, and data collectors is all part of the development and, ideally, procurement process. But due to limited resources, time, and a general failure to imagine all the ways things can go wrong, it is important to monitor the impacts of the data and AI products that are on the market. A car can be built with air bags and crumple zones, but that doesn't mean it's safe to drive it at 100 miles per hour down a side street. Similarly, AI products can be ethically developed but unethically deployed. There is both qualitative and quantitative research to be done here, including especially engaging stakeholders to determine how the product has affected them. Indeed, in the ideal scenario, relevant stakeholders are identified early in the development process and incorporated into an articulation of what the product does and does not do.

Operationalizing data and AI ethics is not an easy task. It requires buy-in from senior leadership and cross-functional collaboration. Companies that make the investment, however, will not only see mitigated risk but also more efficient adoption of the technologies they need to forge ahead. And finally, they'll be exactly what their clients, consumers, and employees are looking for: trustworthy.

Reid Blackman is the author of *Ethical Machines: Your Concise Guide to Totally Unbiased, Transparent, and Respectful AI* (Harvard Business Review Press, 2022) and founder and CEO of Virtue, an ethical risk consultancy.

He is also a senior adviser to the Deloitte AI Institute, previously served on Ernst & Young's AI Advisory Board, and volunteers as the chief ethics officer to the nonprofit Government Blockchain Association. Previously, Reid was a professor of philosophy at Colgate University and the University of North Carolina, Chapel Hill.

CHAPTER 17

AI Can Help Address Inequity— If Companies Earn Users' Trust

by Shunyuan Zhang, Kannan Srinivasan, Param Vir Singh, and Nitin Mehta

Unfortunately, the benefits that AI will bring may not be enjoyed equally. Algorithmic bias—when algorithms produce discriminatory outcomes against certain categories of individuals, typically minorities and women—may also worsen existing social inequalities. From the recidivism prediction algorithm used in courts to the medical

---

Adapted from content posted on hbr.org, September 17, 2021 (product #H06L38).

care prediction algorithm used by hospitals, studies have found evidence of algorithmic biases that make racial disparities worse for those impacted, not better.

Many firms have put considerable effort into combating algorithmic bias in their management and services. They often use data-science driven approaches to investigate what an algorithm's predictions will be before launching it into the world. This can include examining different AI model specifications, defining the objective function that the model should minimize, selecting the input data to be seeded into the model, preprocessing the data, and making post-processing model predictions.

However, the final outcome of deploying an algorithm relies on not only the algorithm predictions but also how it will ultimately be used by business and customers—and this critical context of receptivity and adoption of algorithm is often overlooked. We argue that algorithm deployment must consider the market conditions under which the algorithm is used. Such market conditions may affect what or who, and to what extent, the algorithm's decisions will impact, and hence influence, the realized benefits of using the algorithm.

When Well-Intentioned Algorithms Have Detrimental Effects

For example, to help its hosts maximize their income (i.e., property revenue), Airbnb launched an AI algorithm-based smart-pricing tool that automatically adjusts a listing's daily price. Airbnb hosts have very limited information on competing Airbnb properties, hotel rates, seasonality, and various other demand shocks that they can use to correctly price their properties. The smart-pricing algorithm was meant to help with this, incorporating relevant information on host, property, and neighborhood characteristics from the company's enormous information sources to determine the best price for a property. In our recently published study, the average daily revenue of hosts who adopted smart pricing increased by 8.6%. Nevertheless, after the launch of the algorithm, the racial revenue gap increased (i.e., white hosts earned more) at the population level, which includes both adopters and non-adopters, because Black hosts were significantly less likely to adopt the algorithm than white hosts were.

In tests, the tool did exactly what it was supposed to. We found that it was perfectly race blind in that the prices of similar listings were reduced by the same amount regardless of the race of the host. The algorithm improved revenue for Black hosts more than it did for white hosts. This is because the property demand curve for Black hosts was more elastic (i.e., more responsive to price changes) than the demand curve for equivalent properties owned by white hosts. As the price reduction was the same, the number of bookings increased more for Black hosts than for white ones, leading to a higher increase in revenue for Black hosts than for white hosts. From a data-science perspective, it had a perfect deployment: This race-blind, well-meaning algorithm aimed to provide financial benefits by improving the revenue of all adopters and to deliver social benefits by reducing the racial revenue gap among adopters.

In the real world, however, it was a different story. The algorithm launch ended up widening rather than narrowing the racial disparity on Airbnb. This unintended consequence could have been avoided by internalizing market conditions during algorithm deployment.

We determined that firms must consider the following market conditions during AI algorithm creation: (1) the targeted users' receptivity to an AI algorithm, (2) consumers' reactions to algorithm predictions, and (3) whether the algorithm should be regulated to address racial and economic inequalities by incorporating firms' strategic behavior in developing the algorithm. Airbnb, for example, should have asked: (1) How will Airbnb hosts react to (more specifically, adopt) the algorithm, and (2) how can Black hosts be encouraged to adopt it? These market conditions determine the final market outcome (e.g., product price, property demand, benefits to users) of applying an AI algorithm, and thus should be analyzed and considered upfront.

How Will an Algorithm Be Perceived by the Targeted Users?

Airbnb's smart-pricing algorithm increased daily revenue for everyone who used it. White hosts saw a bump of $5.20 per day, and Black hosts saw a $13.90 increase. The new pricing reduced economic disparity among adopters by 71.3%.

However, as Black hosts were 41% less likely than white hosts to adopt the algorithm, the outcome of the algorithm's introduction was not quite satisfactory. For Black hosts who didn't use the algorithm, the earnings gap actually *increased*. This leads to the following question: If you are the CEO of a company that wishes to root out racial inequity and are given an algorithm report of this kind, what do you hope to encourage in the science and engineering management team?

To address Black hosts' low receptivity to the new tool, for example, Airbnb could encourage Black hosts to adopt the algorithm by rewarding Black users who try it out or sharing a detailed description and evidence of the benefits of using the algorithm. We also found that the racial adoption gap was more significant among hosts with a low socioeconomic status (SES), so targeting Black hosts in the lower SES quartiles would be most efficient.

To do this, however, it's essential to understand why people are hesitant in the first place. There are many reasons why people may not be receptive to handing over control to an algorithm. For example, education and income have been found to explain a high technology adoption barrier for Black users, especially when using the technology is (financially) costly. Even if the technology is offered for free (e.g., Airbnb's smart pricing algorithm), trust also plays a significant role: A working paper (Shunyuan Zhang coauthored with Yang Yang) indicated that raising awareness of racial bias would make disadvantaged groups less trustful and more hesitant to embrace algorithms in general, including the race-blind ones that offer financial, health, or education benefits to the users.[1]

In conversations with an e-commerce company focused on used items, authors of the study learned that only 20% of the sellers used the free pricing tool offered by the company, making pricing inefficient and selling slow. A preliminary survey suggested that sellers may overestimate the value of their used items and may be unwilling to accept algorithm-predicted price suggestions; this is called the endowment effect. For example, imagine a seller lists a secondhand dress they believe is worth $15, but the pricing algorithm, which was trained on an enormous data set and models, suggests $10, and the seller reacts negatively. In response to reactions like this, the company could explain to the seller how the $10 suggestion was made and present similar items that were priced and sold at $10. Providing such explanation increases the transparency of business operations and enhances customer trust.

Simply put, when incorporating differences in the adoption of AI algorithms across racial groups, firms should customize their algorithm promotion efforts and try to address the concerns of the users they most want to adopt it.

How Will Consumers React to the Effects of an AI Algorithm?

It is a mistake to see AI algorithms merely as models that output decisions and impact the people who receive those decisions. The impact goes both ways: How consumers (i.e., decision recipients) react to AI decisions will shape the effect of the algorithm on market outcomes.

Airbnb's smart-pricing algorithm is a good example of this phenomenon. Assume that you are the CEO of

Airbnb and are reporting on the algorithm developed by your company at a House Committee Hearing on equitable AI. You might be happy that your algorithm, conditional on adoption, could combat racial inequity. However, you could do more to mitigate racial disparity. You should consider the following key marketing conditions: (1) Black and white hosts may face different demand curves, and (2) Black hosts are less represented in the data used to train the AI algorithm. Specifically, the demand curve for Black hosts' properties was more elastic than that for similar properties owned by white hosts. Different demand curves might arise from social discrimination, which leads guests to be more price sensitive to Black-owned properties than to white-owned ones.

As guests were more responsive to price reductions for Black-owned properties, incorporating this market condition when deploying an AI algorithm is critical. You can further reduce the revenue gap between Black and white hosts by directly using race or indirectly including closely or correlated characteristics in the algorithm. Ignoring the inherent differences in market conditions may lead to price suggestions that are farther from the optimal prices for Black hosts than from the optimal prices for white hosts. This is because Black hosts represent only 9% of Airbnb properties, whereas white hosts represent 80%.

What Should Firms Do?

If you are on an AI equity task force at the corporate or government level, what should you do when considering how to deploy an algorithm meant to mitigate racial disparities? If you were to sketch the ecosystem of the focal algorithm, who would the creators, the targeted users, and the algorithm decision receivers be? How would they react to the algorithm, and how would their reactions impact the algorithm's final outcome?

First, really consider how the algorithm will be perceived by the targeted users. This will shape how it performs in the real world. Ask whether users are aware (or can be made aware) of how the algorithm works. If they know that your company is deploying a new algorithm meant to address an inequity, how will they react? If underrepresented users may feel pressured or feel that the algorithm may be biased against them, they will be less likely to use it. Take into account how historical discrimination and recent issues with underrepresentation in data sets may make your target users skeptical.

Second, focus on building trust and help users understand *what* the algorithm is meant to do and *how* it works. If algorithm adoption is optional (as in the case of Airbnb), this process of considering whether users—particularly users from underrepresented groups—will understand, trust, and adopt the algorithm is even more important. Communicating clearly with them about the purpose of introducing the algorithm and how it works, as well as incentivizing them to use the algorithm, especially when it is more effective for the minority or gender-based groups, is important. Make explaining how the initiative was launched to reduce racial inequities—and how it will do so—part of your rollout strategy.

Due to the scalability and value of accurate predictions, businesses will increasingly deploy and apply algorithms in their operations and services—and adoption will likely only increase. But companies need to address the concerns that algorithms might produce biased outcomes against the disadvantaged groups. Unfortunately, the common data science–driven approaches including processing data and calibrating model specifications are insufficient and inefficient. For business to best combat algorithmic bias issues, considering the perception and adoption of algorithms and the market conditions like the ones we have described should be a major part of rolling out algorithmic tools.

Done right, these tools may well mitigate the human biases and bridge the economic consequences arising from them. Done wrong, just by a few algorithms from established firms, may completely undermine and slow the AI algorithm deployment.

Shunyuan Zhang is an assistant professor in the marketing unit at Harvard Business School. She conducts analyses of structured and unstructured data generated by new sharing economy platforms to address important issues emerging in the sharing economy. Her recent research interests include studying economic implications of algorithm predictions and algorithmic bias on individuals' receptivity of algorithms, equity across heterogeneous users, and platform competitions. **Kannan Srinivasan** is the H. J. Heinz II Professor of Management,

Marketing and Business Technologies at the Tepper School of Business, Carnegie Mellon University. Previously, he taught at the business schools at Stanford and the University of Chicago. He has worked on quantifying the economic value of unstructured data (including text and images) combining deep learning and econometric methods. Recently, he has been working in areas such as scalability of cryptocurrency, the sharing economy, algorithm bias in artificial intelligence, and beneficial effects of ad-blockers. **Param Vir Singh** is the Carnegie Bosch Professor of Business Technologies and Marketing at the Tepper School of Business, Carnegie Mellon University. Singh's recent research focuses on artificial intelligence and the economic implications of algorithmic bias, transparency, and interpretability to businesses and society. His work has appeared in *Marketing Science, Management Science, Information Systems Research*, and *Organization Science*. He is a senior editor at *Information Systems Research* and an associate editor at *Management Science*. **Nitin Mehta** is a professor of marketing and the area coordinator of marketing at the University of Toronto. His research focuses on structural models of consumer search, multicategory choices, imperfect recall and learning, consumers' health care decisions, adoption of AI by firms and consumers, and the societal impact of AI. Nitin has taught the core MBA marketing course for many years and is currently teaching pricing and analytics for marketing strategy. He is currently serving as the associate editor at *Marketing Science* and *International Journal of Research in Marketing*.

NOTE

1. Shunyuan Zhang and Yang Yang, "The Unintended Consequences of Raising Awareness: Knowing About the Existence of Algorithmic Racial Bias Widens Racial Inequality," working paper 22-017, Harvard Business School, Boston, 2021.

CHAPTER 18

Take Action to Mitigate Ethical Risks

by Reid Blackman and Beena Ammanath

Over the past several years, concerns around AI ethics have gone mainstream. The concerns, and the outcomes everyone wants to avoid, are largely agreed upon and well documented. No one wants to push out discriminatory or biased AI. No one wants to be the object of a lawsuit or regulatory investigation for violations of privacy. But once we've all agreed that biased, black-box, privacy-violating AI is bad, where do we go from here?

Adapted from "Ethics and AI: 3 Conversations Companies Need to Have," on hbr.org, March 21, 2022 (product #H06VL0).

The question most every senior leader asks is: How do we take action to mitigate those ethical risks?

Acting quickly to address concerns is admirable, but with the complexities of machine learning, ethics, and their points of intersection, there are no quick fixes. To implement, scale, and maintain effective AI ethical risk-mitigation strategies, companies should begin with a deep understanding of the problems they're trying to solve. A challenge, however, is that conversations about AI ethics can feel nebulous. The first step, then, should consist of learning how to talk about these in concrete, actionable ways. Here's how you can set the table to have AI ethics conversations in a way that can make next steps clear.

Who Needs to Be Involved?

We recommend assembling a senior-level working group that will be responsible for driving AI ethics in your organization. They should have the right skills, experience, and knowledge to ensure that the conversations are well informed about the business needs, technical capacities, and operational know-how. At a minimum, we recommend involving four kinds of people: technologists, legal/compliance experts, ethicists, and business leaders who understand the problems you're trying to solve using AI. Their collective goal is to understand the sources of ethical risks generally, for the industry of which they are members, and for their particular company. After all, there are no good solutions without a deep understanding of the problem itself and the potential obstacles for proposed solutions.

You need the technologist to assess what is technologically feasible, not only at a per-product level but also at an organizational level. That is because, in part, various ethical risk-mitigation plans require different tech tools and skills. Knowing where your organization is from a technological perspective can be essential to mapping out how to identify and close the biggest gaps.

Legal and compliance experts are there to help ensure that any new risk-mitigation plan is compatible and not redundant with existing risk-mitigation practices. Legal issues loom particularly large in light of the fact that it's neither clear how existing laws and regulations bear on new technologies nor what new regulations or laws are coming down the pipeline.

Ethicists are there to help ensure a systematic and thorough investigation into the ethical and reputational risks you face not only by virtue of developing and procuring AI but also those that are particular to your industry and/or your organization. Ethicists' importance is particularly relevant because compliance with outdated regulations does not ensure the ethical and reputational safety of your organization.

Finally, business leaders should help ensure that all risk is mitigated in a way that is compatible with business necessities and goals. Zero risk is an impossibility so long as anyone does anything. But unnecessary risk is a threat to the bottom line, and risk-mitigation strategies also should be chosen with an eye toward what is economically feasible.

Three Conversations to Push Things Forward

Once the team is in place, here are three crucial conversations to have.

Define your organization's ethical standard for AI

Any conversation should recognize that legal compliance (e.g., anti-discrimination law) and regulatory compliance (with, say, GDPR and/or CCPA) are table stakes. The question to address is: Given that the set of ethical risks is not identical to the set of legal/regulatory risks, what do we identify as the ethical risks for our industry/organization and where do we stand on them?

There are a lot of tough questions that need answers here. For instance, what, by your organization's lights, counts as a discriminatory model? Suppose, for instance, your AI hiring software discriminates against women, but it discriminates *less* than they've been historically discriminated against. Is your benchmark for sufficiently unbiased "better than humans have done in the last 10 years"? Or is there some other benchmark you think is appropriate? Those in the self-driving car sector know this question well: "Do we deploy self-driving cars at scale when they are better than the average human driver or when they are at least as good as (or better than) our best human drivers?"

Similar questions arise in the context of black-box models. Where does your organization stand on explainability? Are there cases in which you find using a black box acceptable (e.g., so long as it tests well against your chosen benchmark)? What are the criteria for determining whether an AI with explainable outputs is otiose, nice-to-have, or need-to-have?

Going deep on these questions allows you to develop frameworks and tools for your product teams and the executives who greenlight deployment of the product. For instance, you may decide that every product must go through an ethical risk due diligence process before being deployed or even at the earliest stages of product design. You may also settle on guidelines regarding when, if at any time, black-box models may be used. Getting to a point where you can articulate the minimum ethical standards that all AI must meet is a good sign that progress has been made. Guidelines are also important for gaining the trust of customers and clients, and they demonstrate your due diligence has been performed should regulators investigate whether your organization has deployed a discriminatory model.

Identify the gaps between where you are now and what your standards call for

There are various technical "solutions" or "fixes" to AI ethics problems. A number of software products from big tech to startups to nonprofits help data scientists apply quantitative metrics of fairness to their model outputs. Tools like LIME and SHAP aid data scientists in explaining how outputs are arrived at in the first place. But virtually no one thinks these technical solutions, or any technological solution for that matter, will sufficiently mitigate the ethical risk and transform your organization into one that meets its AI ethics standards.

Your AI ethics team should determine where its respective limits are and how its skills and knowledge can complement each other. This means asking:

1. What, exactly, is the risk we're trying to mitigate?

2. How does software/quantitative analysis help us mitigate that risk?

3. What gaps do the software/quantitative analyses leave?

4. What kinds of qualitative assessments do we need to make, when do we need to make them, on what basis do we make them, and who should make them, so that those gaps are appropriately filled?

These conversations should also include a crucial piece that is standardly left out: What level of technological maturity is needed to satisfy (some) ethical demands (e.g., whether you have the technological capacity to provide explanations that are needed in the context of deep neural networks). Having productive conversations about what AI ethical risk-management goals are achievable requires keeping an eye on what is technologically feasible for your organization.

Answers to these questions can provide clear guidance on next steps: Assess what quantitative solutions can be dovetailed with existing practices by product teams, assess the organization's capacity for the qualitative assessments, and assess how, in your organization, these things can be married effectively and seamlessly.

Understand the complex sources of the problems and operationalize solutions

Many conversations around bias in AI start with giving examples and immediately talking about "biased data sets." Sometimes this will slide into talk about "implicit bias" or "unconscious bias," which are terms borrowed from psychology that lack a clear and direct application to "biased data sets." But it's not enough to say, "the models are trained on biased data sets" or "the AI reflects our historical societal discriminatory actions and policies."

The issue isn't that these things aren't (sometimes, often) true; it's that it cannot be the whole picture. Understanding bias in AI requires, for instance, talking about the various sources of discriminatory outputs. That can be the result of the training data; but *how*, exactly, those data sets can be biased is important, if for no other reason than that how they are biased informs how you determine the optimal bias-mitigation strategy. Other issues abound: how inputs are weighted, where thresholds are set, and what objective function is chosen. In short, the conversation around discriminatory algorithms has to go deep around the *multiple* sources of the problem and how those sources connect to various risk-mitigation strategies.

Productive conversations on ethics should go deeper than broad-stroke examples decried by specialists and nonspecialists alike. Your organization needs the right people at the table so that its standards can be defined and deepened. Your organization should fruitfully marry its quantitative and qualitative approaches to ethical risk mitigation so it can close the gaps between where it is now and where it wants it to be. And it should appreciate the complexity of the sources of its AI ethical risks. At the end of the day, AI ethical risk isn't nebulous or theoretical. It's concrete. And it deserves and requires a level of attention that goes well beyond the repetition of scary headlines.

Reid Blackman is the author of *Ethical Machines: Your Concise Guide to Totally Unbiased, Transparent, and Respectful AI* (Harvard Business Review Press, 2022) and the founder and CEO of Virtue, an ethical risk consultancy. He is also a senior adviser to the Deloitte AI Institute, previously served on Ernst & Young's AI Advisory Board, and volunteers as the chief ethics officer to the nonprofit Government Blockchain Association. Previously, Reid was a professor of philosophy at Colgate University and the University of North Carolina, Chapel Hill. **Beena Ammanath** is the Executive Director of the global Deloitte AI Institute, author of *Trustworthy AI*, founder of the nonprofit Humans For AI, and also leads trustworthy and ethical tech for Deloitte. She is an award-winning senior executive with extensive global experience in AI and digital transformation, spanning across e-commerce, finance, marketing, telecom, retail, software products, services, and industrial domains with companies such as HPE, GE, Thomson Reuters, British Telecom, Bank of America, and e*trade.

SECTION SIX

Taking the Next Steps with AI and Machine Learning

CHAPTER 19

How No-Code Platforms Can Bring AI to Small and Midsize Businesses

by Jonathon Reilly

Technology often follows a familiar progression. First, it's used by a small core of scientists, then the user base expands to engineers who can navigate technical nuance and jargon until finally it's made user-friendly enough that almost anyone can use it.

Adapted from content posted on hbr.org, November 5, 2021 (product #H06OHE).

Right now, the process for building software is making that final leap. Just as the clickable icons of Windows and Mac OS replaced obscure DOS commands, new "no-code" platforms are replacing programming languages with simple drag-and-drop interfaces. The implications are huge: Where it used to require a team of engineers to build a piece of software, now users with a web browser and an idea have the power to bring that idea to life themselves. This means that powerful tech, which only large, well-resourced businesses have been able to afford, is suddenly within the reach of even small companies.

Perhaps most significantly, this is making it possible to deploy artificial intelligence without hiring an army of expensive developers and data scientists. That means that smaller businesses, which often have huge amounts of data, can employ the benefits of AI, such as powering new kinds of customer experiences (like a self-driving Tesla), growing companies' top line (like P&G's AI-driven advertising spend), and optimizing operations for maximum efficiency (like Walmart's supply chain).

For smaller businesses, knowing where and how to deploy this tech can be daunting. Following in the footsteps of larger companies, which may have already gone through the process of figuring out how data science might work for them, it makes sense to begin by deploying no-code AI on bite-sized tasks as opposed to ocean-boiling mega-projects. Ideally, you want to:

- Work with the data you already have. There is often more value to be captured there than you may initially think.

- Pick high-value tasks in which being more efficient will drive growth.

- Get quick wins in common areas, such as sales funnel optimization or churn reduction, so your team can learn how AI applies to a wide range of use cases.

- Don't be afraid to move on quickly if you cannot achieve a 10x ROI from any AI project. There are plenty of high-return applications.

No-code tools empower employees to think about creative ways to use data to drive or optimize their work—and consequently, the business.

Consider an example like intelligent lead scoring. Sales teams collect leads from all kinds of places—web scraping, cold calling, online forms, business cards dropped in a bowl at a trade show. But once a team has thousands of leads, the problem is deciding which ones to chase down. By spotting patterns in user behavior, demographics, and firmographics, a simple no-code classification model, for example, can rank leads according to their probability of turning into sales—a task for which many large firms use AI.

Using a no-code AI platform, a user can drag and drop a spreadsheet of data about sales prospects into the interface, make a few selections from a drop-down menu, and click on a couple of buttons and the platforms will build a model and return a spreadsheet with leads sorted, from the hottest to the coldest, enabling salespeople to maximize revenue by focusing on the prospects that are most likely to buy.

The potential of AI is everywhere in the enterprise, and the advantage of no-code platforms is that they are not restricted to any particular use case. These tools can be used to detect machine maintenance patterns and predict which machines need attention before they fail, used by marketing teams to spot dissatisfaction and reduce churn, or by operations teams to reduce employee attrition. They can spot patterns in text, not just numbers, and be used to analyze sales notes and transcripts alongside sales history and marketing data, allowing companies to automate complex processes.

For many companies, working with no-code platforms will come down to simply finding the right project—and the right platform.

Where to Start with No-Code

A competent no-code platform needs three critical features.

First, it needs a simple interface that makes it easy to get data into the model training process. That means integrating with today's popular business systems, such as customer relationship management systems like Salesforce, and spreadsheet software, such as Excel. If relevant data lives in multiple places, the platform should be able to merge it.

Once the data is uploaded, the platform needs to be able to automatically classify and correctly encode the data for the model training process—all with minimal input from the user. For example, the platform might identify columns in the data as categories, dates, or numbers and the user should check to see that the columns are labeled correctly.

Second, the platform needs to automate model selection and training—tasks that would normally be performed by data scientists. There are many machine learning approaches, and each works best on a specific type of problem. The platform should have a search mechanism to find the best model based on the data and the prediction required. The user should not need to know their way around regression or k-nearest neighbor algorithms. The platform should just deliver what works best.

Finally, it needs to be simple and easy to deploy with existing processes. A platform should be able to monitor model performance over time and retrain as the business environment shifts and new data becomes available.

How to Pick the Right No-Code Platform

Not all no-code AI platforms are made the same, and the right tool depends on a company's business needs. Solutions range from just a few dollars a month to enterprise platforms that cost six figures a year.

Finding the right one for a particular company may require some trial and error. The good news is that the best platforms are open, which means that anyone can try them to see how they work. In other words, users can take the platforms for test drives on relevant tasks and see how they perform.

For example, users can compare the accuracy of various platforms based on their relative performance on public data sets, such as the Australian credit approval data set where the goal is to classify credit card eligibility. With minimal effort, users can see how often each no-code AI platform is correct when it predicts an outcome in the validation set—a random selection of training data, typically 20%, that is held back and run against the model to measure performance.

But accuracy can sometimes be misleading. It's also important to consider the number of false positives and false negatives in prediction results. This is particularly important for "imbalanced" data sets, where only a small number of cases, like credit card fraud or cancer, need to be detected within large amounts of data.

For example, if a model to predict credit card fraud said "no fraud" every time, it would have very high accuracy but would be useless. A good no-code platform will score false positives and false negatives.

Users should also consider the time it takes to use these no-code platforms. One key metric is the time it takes the platforms to train their models. That can vary from minutes to hours, and if it takes hours, it won't fit easily into a busy person's day.

Training is not the only time consideration. For these platforms to be truly transformative in an organization, they must be so simple to use that nontechnical people will adopt them into their workflows. Check the onboarding processes of various platforms. If it takes help from the IT department or even significant effort, the people in sales or accounting aren't likely to bother.

For more companies to wield the power of AI in more applications across their business, the answer can't be "create and hire more data scientists." As little as one-quarter of 1% of the world knows how to code. Yet, as tech investor Marc Andreessen wrote presciently a decade ago, software is eating the world. There's no doubt that no-code is the future.

Someday every part of every business will be AI optimized. The data is there today. The rate of progress and maturation of the platforms that let more and more people turn that data into AI-driven prediction and optimization machines will determine the speed at which it happens.

Removing friction from adoption will help unleash the power of AI across all industries and allow non-specialists to literally predict the future. In time, no-code AI platforms will be as ubiquitous as word-processing or spreadsheet software is today.

Jonathon Reilly is a cofounder of Akkio, a no-code AI platform.

CHAPTER 20

The Power of Natural Language Processing

by Ross Gruetzemacher

Until recently, the conventional wisdom was that while AI was better than humans at data-driven, decision-making tasks, it was still inferior to humans for cognitive and creative ones. But since 2020, language-based AI has advanced by leaps and bounds, changing common notions of what this technology can do.

The most visible advances have been in what's called "natural language processing" (NLP), the branch of AI

Adapted from content posted on hbr.org, April 19, 2022 (product #H06ZS3).

focused on how computers can process language like humans do. It has been used to write an article for the *Guardian*, and AI-authored blog posts have gone viral—feats that weren't possible a few years ago. AI even excels at cognitive tasks like programming, where it is able to generate programs for simple video games from human instructions.

Yet while these stunts may be attention grabbing, are they really indicative of what this tech can do for businesses?

What NLP Can Do

The best-known natural language processing tool as of writing is GPT-3, from OpenAI, which uses AI and statistics to predict the next word in a sentence based on the preceding words. NLP practitioners call tools like this "language models," and they can be used for simple analytics tasks, such as classifying documents and analyzing the sentiment in blocks of text, as well as more advanced tasks, such as answering questions and summarizing reports. Language models are already reshaping traditional text analytics, but GPT-3 was an especially pivotal language model because, at 10 times larger than any previous model upon release, it was the first *large language model*, which enabled it to perform even more advanced tasks like programming and solving high school–level math problems. The latest version, called InstructGPT, has been fine-tuned by humans to generate responses that are much better aligned with human values and user intentions, and

Google's latest model shows further impressive breakthroughs on language and reasoning.

For businesses, the three areas where GPT-3 has appeared most promising are writing, coding, and discipline-specific reasoning. OpenAI, the Microsoft-funded creator of GPT-3, has developed a GPT-3-based language model intended to act as an assistant for programmers by generating code from natural language input. This tool, Codex, is already powering products like Copilot for Microsoft's subsidiary GitHub and is capable of creating a basic video game simply by typing instructions. This transformative capability was already expected to change the nature of how programmers do their jobs, but models continue to improve—the latest from Google's DeepMind AI lab, for example, demonstrates the critical thinking and logic skills necessary to outperform most humans in programming competitions.

Models like GPT-3 are considered to be foundation models—an emerging AI research area—which also work for other types of data such as images and video. Foundation models can even be trained on multiple forms of data at the same time, like OpenAI's DALL·E 2, which is trained on language and images to generate high-resolution renderings of imaginary scenes or objects simply from text prompts. Due to their potential to transform the nature of cognitive work, economists expect that foundation models may affect every part of the economy and could lead to increases in economic growth similar to the Industrial Revolution.

How Can Organizations Prepare for the Future?

Identify your text data assets and determine how the latest techniques can be leveraged to add value for your firm

You are certainly aware of the value of data, but you still may be overlooking some essential data assets if you are not utilizing text analytics and NLP throughout your organization. Text data is certainly valuable for customer experience management and understanding the voice of the customer but think about other text data assets in your organization: emails, analysts' reports, contracts, press releases, archives—even meetings and phone calls can be transcribed.

There is so much text data, and you don't need advanced models like GPT-3 to extract its value. Hugging Face, an NLP startup, released AutoNLP, a tool that automates training models for standard text analytics tasks by simply uploading your data to the platform. The data still needs labels but far fewer than in other applications. Because many firms have made ambitious bets on AI only to struggle to drive value into the core business, remain cautious. This can be a good first step that your existing machine learning engineers—or even talented data scientists—can manage.

To take the next step, again, identify your data assets. Many sectors, and even divisions within your organization, use highly specialized vocabularies. Through a combination of your data assets and open data sets, train a model for the needs of specific sectors or divisions.

Think of finance. You do not want a model specialized in finance. You want a model customized for commercial banking or for capital markets. Specialized models can unlock untold value for your firm.

Understand how you might leverage AI-based language technologies to make better decisions or reorganize your skilled labor

Language-based AI won't replace jobs, but it will automate many tasks, even for decision-makers. Startups like Verneek are creating Elicit-like tools to enable everyone to make data-informed decisions. These new tools will transcend traditional business intelligence and will transform the nature of many roles in organizations—programmers are just the beginning.

You need to start understanding how these technologies can be used to reorganize your skilled labor. The next generation of tools like OpenAI's Codex will lead to more productive programmers, which likely means fewer dedicated programmers and more employees with modest programming skills using them for an increasing number of more complex tasks. This may not be true for all software developers, but it has significant implications for tasks like data processing and web development.

Begin incorporating new language-based AI tools for a variety of tasks to better understand their capabilities

Tools like Elicit are just emerging, but they can already be useful in surprising ways. In fact, the previous suggestion was inspired by one of Elicit's brainstorming tasks conditioned on my other three suggestions. The original suggestion itself wasn't perfect, but it reminded me of some critical topics that I had overlooked, and I revised the article accordingly. In organizations, tasks like this can assist strategic thinking or scenario-planning exercises. Although there is tremendous potential for such applications, right now the results are still relatively crude, but they can already add value in their current state.

The bottom line is that you need to encourage broad adoption of language-based AI tools throughout your business. It is difficult to anticipate just how these tools might be used at different levels of your organization, but the best way to get an understanding of this tech may be for you and other leaders in your firm to adopt it yourselves. Don't bet the boat on it because some of the tech may not work out, but if your team gains a better understanding of what is possible, then you will be ahead of the competition. Remember that while current AI might not be poised to replace managers, managers who understand AI are poised to replace managers who don't.

Do not underestimate the transformative potential of AI

Large foundation models like GPT-3 exhibit abilities to generalize to a large number of tasks without any task-specific training. The recent progress in this tech is a significant step toward the human-level generalization and general artificial intelligence that are the ultimate goals of many AI researchers, including those at OpenAI and Google's DeepMind. Such systems have tremendous disruptive potential that could lead to AI-driven explosive economic growth, which would radically transform business and society. While you may still be skeptical of radically transformative AI like artificial general intelligence, it is prudent for organizations' leaders to be cognizant of early signs of progress due to its tremendous disruptive potential.

Consider that former Google chief Eric Schmidt expects general artificial intelligence in 10–20 years and that the United Kingdom recently took an official position on risks from artificial general intelligence. Ignoring the transformative potential of AI also carries risks: Firms' inaction or irresponsible use of AI could have widespread and damaging effects on society (e.g., increasing inequality or domain-specific risks from automation). Organizations should begin preparing now not only to capitalize on transformative AI but to do their part to avoid undesirable futures and ensure that advanced AI is used to equitably benefit society.

Language-Based AI Tools Are Here to Stay

Powerful generalizable language-based AI tools like Elicit are here, and they are just the tip of the iceberg; multimodal foundation model-based tools are poised to transform business in ways that are still difficult to predict. To begin preparing now, start understanding your text data assets and the variety of cognitive tasks involved in different roles in your organization. Aggressively adopt new language-based AI technologies; some will work well and others will not, but your employees will be quicker to adjust when you move on to the next.

And don't forget to adopt these technologies yourself—this is the best way for you to start to understand their future roles in your organization.

Ross Gruetzemacher is an assistant professor of business analytics at the W. Frank Barton School of Business at Wichita State University. He is a consultant on AI strategy for organizations in the Bay Area and internationally, and he also works as a senior game master on *Intelligence Rising*, a strategic role-play game for exploring AI futures.

CHAPTER 21

Reinforcement Learning Is Ready for Business

by Kathryn Hume and Matthew E. Taylor

Lee Sedol, a world-class Go champion, was flummoxed by the 37th move Deepmind's AlphaGo made in the second match of the famous 2016 series. So flummoxed that it took him nearly 15 minutes to formulate a response. The move was strange to other experienced Go players as well, with one commentator suggesting it was a mistake. In fact, it was a canonical example of an artificial intelligence algorithm learning something that seemed to go beyond just pattern recognition in data—learning something strategic and even creative. Indeed, beyond

---

Adapted from "Why AI That Teaches Itself to Achieve a Goal Is the Next Big Thing," on hbr.org, April 21, 2021 (product #H06BMZ).

just feeding the algorithm past examples of Go champions playing games, Deepmind developers trained AlphaGo by having it play many millions of matches against itself. During these matches, the system had the chance to explore new moves and strategies, and then evaluate if they improved performance. Through all this trial and error, it discovered a way to play the game that surprised even the best players in the world.

If this kind of AI with creative capabilities seems different than the chatbots and predictive models most businesses end up with when they apply machine learning, that's because it is. Instead of machine learning that uses historical data to generate predictions, game-playing systems like AlphaGo use reinforcement learning—a mature machine learning technology that's good at optimizing tasks. To do so, an agent takes a series of actions over time, and each action is informed by the outcome of the previous ones. Put simply, it works by trying different approaches and latching onto—reinforcing—the ones that seem to work better than the others. With enough trials, you can reinforce your way to beating your current best approach and discover a new best way to accomplish your task.

Despite its demonstrated usefulness, however, reinforcement learning is mostly used in academia and niche areas like video games and robotics. Companies such as Netflix, Spotify, and Google have started using it, but most businesses lag behind. Yet opportunities are everywhere. In fact, any time you have to make decisions in sequence—what AI practitioners call sequential decision tasks—there is a chance to deploy reinforcement learning.

Consider the many real-world problems that require deciding how to act over time, where there is something to maximize (or minimize), and where you're never explicitly given the correct solution. For example:

- How should you route data traffic to different servers or decide what servers to power down in a data center?

- When building a molecule in simulation to develop a breakthrough drug, how do you determine which reagent to add next?

- If you want to sell a large amount of stock, how do you carefully sell small orders throughout a day to minimize the amount that the stock price drops?

If you're a company leader, there are likely many processes you'd like to automate or optimize, but that are too dynamic or have too many exceptions and edge cases, to program into software. Through trial and error, reinforcement learning algorithms can learn to solve even the most dynamic optimization problems—opening up new avenues for automation and personalization in quickly changing environments.

What Reinforcement Learning Can Do

Many businesses think of machine learning systems as "prediction machines" and apply algorithms to forecast things like cash flow or customer attrition based on data such as transaction patterns or website analytics behavior. These systems tend to use what's called supervised machine learning. With supervised learning, you typically make a *prediction*: The stock will likely go up by four points in the next six hours. Then, after you make that prediction, you're given the actual answer: The stock actually went up by three points. The system learns by updating its mapping between input data—like past prices of the same stock and perhaps of other equities and indicators—and output prediction to better match the actual answer, which is called the ground truth.

With reinforcement learning, however, there's no correct answer to learn from. Reinforcement learning systems produce actions, not predictions—they'll suggest the action most likely to maximize (or minimize) a metric. They observe how well they did on a particular task and whether it was done faster or more efficiently than before. Because these systems learn through trial and error, they work best when they can rapidly try an action (or sequence of actions) and get feedback—a stock market algorithm that takes hundreds of actions per day is a good use case; optimizing customer lifetime value over the course of five years, with only irregular interaction points, is not. Significantly, because of how they learn, they don't need mountains of historical data—they'll experiment and create their own data along the way.

They can therefore be used to *automate* a process, like placing items into a shipping container with a robotic arm, or to *optimize* a process, like deciding when and through what channel to contact a client who missed a payment for the highest recouped revenue and lowest expended effort. In either case, designing the inputs, actions, and rewards the system uses is the key—it will optimize exactly what you encode it to optimize and doesn't do well with any ambiguity.

Google's use of reinforcement learning to help cool its data centers is a good example of how this technology can be applied. Servers in data centers generate a lot of heat, especially when they're in close proximity to one another, and overheating can lead to IT performance issues or equipment damage. In this use case, the input data is various measurements about the environment, like air pressure and temperature. The actions are fan speed (which controls air flow) and valve opening (the amount of water used) in air-handling units. The system includes some rules to follow, such as safe operating guidelines, and it sequences how air flows through the center to keep the temperature at a specified level while minimizing energy usage. The physical dynamics of a data center environment are complex and constantly changing; a shift in the weather impacts temperature and humidity, and each physical location often has a unique architecture and setup. Reinforcement learning algorithms are able to pick up on nuances that would be too hard to describe with formulas and rules.

Here at Borealis AI, we partnered with Royal Bank of Canada's Capital Markets business to develop a reinforcement learning-based trade execution system called Aiden. Aiden's objective is to execute a customer's stock order (to buy or sell a certain number of shares) within a specified time window, seeking prices that minimize loss relative to a specified benchmark. This becomes a sequential decision task because of the detrimental market impact of buying or selling too many shares at once: The task is to sequence actions throughout the day to minimize price impact.

The stock market is dynamic and the performance of traditional algorithms (the rules-based algorithms traders have used for years) can vary when today's market conditions differ from yesterday's. We felt this was a good reinforcement learning opportunity—it had the right balance between clarity and dynamic complexity. We could clearly enumerate the different actions Aiden could take, and the reward we wanted to optimize (minimize the difference between the prices Aiden achieved and the market volume-weighted average price benchmark). The stock market moves fast and generates a lot of data, giving the algorithm quick iterations to learn.

We let the algorithm do just that through countless simulations before launching the system live to the market. Ultimately, Aiden proved able to perform well during some of the more volatile market periods during the beginning of the Covid-19 pandemic—conditions that are particularly tough for predictive AIs. It was able to adapt to the changing environment, while continuing to stay close to its benchmark target.

How to Spot an Opportunity for Reinforcement Learning

How can you tell if you're overlooking a problem that reinforcement learning might be able to fix? Here's where to start:

Make a list

Create an inventory of business processes that involve a sequence of steps, and clearly state what you want to maximize or minimize. Focus on processes with dense, frequent actions and opportunities for feedback, and avoid processes with infrequent actions and where it's difficult to observe which worked best to collect feedback. Getting the objective right will likely require iteration.

Consider other options

Don't start with reinforcement learning if you can tackle a problem with other machine learning or optimization techniques. Reinforcement learning is helpful when you lack sufficient historical data to train an algorithm. You need to explore options (and create data along the way).

Be careful what you wish for

If you do want to move ahead, domain experts should closely collaborate with technical teams to help design the inputs, actions, and rewards. For inputs, seek the smallest set of information you could use to make a good decision. For actions, ask how much flexibility you want to give the system; start simple and later expand the range of actions. For rewards, think carefully about the outcomes—and be cautious to avoid falling into the traps of considering one variable in isolation or opting for short-term gains with long-term pains.

Ask whether it's worth it

Will the possible gains justify the costs for development? Many companies need to make digital transformation investments to have the systems and dense, data-generating business processes in place to really make reinforcement learning systems useful. To understand whether the investment will pay off, technical teams should take stock of computational resources to ensure you have the compute power required to support trials and allow the system to explore and identify the optimal sequence. (They may want to create a simulation environment to test the algorithm before releasing it live.) On the software front, if you're planning to use a learning system for customer engagement, you need to have a system that can support A/B testing. This is critical to the learning process, as the algorithm needs to explore different options before it can latch onto which one works best. Finally, if your technology stack can only release features universally, you likely need to upgrade before you start optimizing.

Prepare to be patient

And last but not least, as with many learning algorithms, you have to be open to errors early on while the system learns. It won't find the optimal path from day one, but it will get there in time—and potentially find surprising, creative solutions beyond human imagination when it does.

While reinforcement learning is a mature technology, it's only now starting to be applied in business settings. The technology shines when used to automate or optimize business processes that generate dense data, and where there could be unanticipated changes you couldn't capture with formulas or rules. If you can spot an opportunity, and either lean on an in-house technical team or partner with experts in the space, you may have a window of time to apply this technology and outpace your competition.

Kathryn Hume is the Vice President of Digital Investments Technology at the Royal Bank of Canada. Prior to joining RBC, Hume held leadership positions at Integrate.ai and Fast Forward Labs, where she helped over 50 *Fortune* 500 organizations develop and implement AI programs. She has taught courses on digital transformation and legal ethics at the business and law schools at Harvard, MIT, the University of Toronto, and the University of Calgary. **Matthew E. Taylor** is an associate professor of computing science at the University of Alberta, where he directs the Intelligent Robot LearningLab, and is a fellow and fellow-in-residence at Amii (the Alberta Machine Intelligence Institute). His current research interests include fundamental improvements to reinforcement learning, applying reinforcement learning to real-world problems, and human-AI interaction. He is a coauthor of *Applying Reinforcement Learning Real-World Data with Practical Examples in Python*, which is aimed at practitioners without degrees in machine learning.

EPILOGUE

Scaling AI

CHAPTER 22

How to Scale AI in Your Organization

by Manasi Vartak

AI is most valuable when it is operationalized at scale. For business leaders who wish to maximize business value using AI, *scale* refers to how deeply and widely AI is integrated into an organization's core product or service and business processes.

Unfortunately, scaling AI in this sense isn't easy. Getting one or two AI models into production is very different from running an entire enterprise or product on AI. And as AI is scaled, problems can (and often do) scale, too. For example, one financial company lost $20,000 in 10 minutes because one of its machine learning models began to misbehave. With no visibility into the root

---

Adapted from content posted on hbr.org, March 4, 2022.

issue—and no way to even identify which of its models was malfunctioning—the company was left with no choice but to pull the plug. All models were rolled back to much earlier iterations, which severely degraded performance and erased weeks of effort.

Organizations that are serious about AI have started to adopt a new discipline, defined loosely as machine learning operations (MLOps). MLOps seeks to establish best practices and tools to facilitate rapid, safe, and efficient development and operationalization of AI. When implemented right, MLOps can significantly accelerate the speed to market. Implementing MLOps requires investing time and resources in three key areas: processes, people, and tools.

Processes: Standardize How You Build and Operationalize Models

Building the models and algorithms that power AI is a creative process that requires constant iteration and refinement. Data scientists prepare the data, create features, train the model, tune its parameters, and validate that it works. When the model is ready to be deployed, software engineers and IT operationalize it, monitoring the output and performance continually to ensure the model works robustly in production. Finally, a governance team needs to oversee the entire process to ensure that the AI model being built is sound from an ethics and compliance standpoint.

Given the complexity involved here, the first step to making AI scale is standardization: a way to build models in a repeatable fashion and a well-defined process to operationalize them. In this way, creating AI is closely akin to manufacturing: The first widget a company makes is always bespoke; scaling the manufacturing to produce lots of widgets and then optimizing their design continuously is where a repeatable development and manufacturing process becomes essential. But with AI, many companies struggle with this process.

It's easy to see why. Bespoke processes are (by nature) fraught with inefficiency. Yet many organizations fall into the trap of reinventing the wheel every time they operationalize a model. In the case of the financial company discussed above, the lack of a repeatable way to monitor model performance caused expensive and slow-to-remedy failures. One-off processes like these can spell big trouble once research models are released into production.

The process standardization piece of MLOps helps streamline development, implementation, and refinement of models, enabling teams to build AI capabilities in a rapid but responsible manner.

To standardize, organizations should collaboratively define a "recommended" process for AI development and operationalization and provide tools to support the adoption of that process. For example, the organization can develop a standard set of libraries to validate AI models, thus encouraging consistent testing and validation. Standardization at handoff points in the AI lifecycle (e.g., from data science to IT) is particularly important, as it allows different teams to work independently and focus on their core competencies without worrying about unexpected, disruptive changes.

MLOps tools such as Model Catalogs and Feature Stores can support this standardization.

People: Let Teams Focus on What They're Best At

AI development used to be the responsibility of an AI "data science" team, but building AI at scale can't be done by a single team—it requires a variety of unique skill sets, and very few individuals possess all of them. For example, a data scientist creates algorithmic models that can accurately and consistently predict behavior, while an ML engineer optimizes, packages, and integrates research models into products and monitors their quality on an ongoing basis. One individual will seldom fulfill both roles well. Compliance, governance, and risk requires an even more distinct set of skills. As AI is scaled, more and more expertise is required.

To successfully scale AI, business leaders should build and empower specialized, dedicated teams that can focus on high-value strategic priorities that only their team can accomplish. Let data scientists do data science; let engineers do the engineering; let IT focus on infrastructure.

Two team structures have emerged as organizations scale their AI footprint. First, there is the "pod model," where AI product development is undertaken by a small team made up of a data scientist, data engineer, and ML or software engineer. The second, the "Center of Excellence" or COE model, is when the organization pools together all its data science experts, who are then assigned to different product teams depending on requirements and resource availability. Both approaches have been implemented successfully and come with different pros and cons. The pod model is best suited for fast execution but can lead to knowledge siloes, whereas the COE model has the opposite tradeoff. In contrast to data science and IT, governance teams are most effective when they sit outside of the pods and COEs.

Tools: Pick Tools That Support Creativity, Speed, and Safety

Finally, we come to tools. Given that trying to standardize production of AI and ML is a relatively new project, the ecosystem of data science and machine learning tools is highly fragmented—to build a single model, a data scientist works with roughly a dozen different, highly specialized tools and stitches them together. On the other side, IT or governance uses a completely different set of tools, and these distinct tool chains don't easily talk to each other. As a result, it's easy to do one-off work, but building a robust, repeatable workflow is difficult.

Ultimately, this limits the speed at which AI can be scaled across an organization. A scattershot collection of tools can lead to long times to market and AI products being built without adequate oversight.

But as AI scales across an organization, collaboration becomes more fundamental to success. Faster iteration demands ongoing contributions from stakeholders across the model lifecycle, and finding the correct tool or platform is an essential step. Tools and platforms that support AI at scale must support creativity, speed, and safety. Without the right tools in place, a business will struggle to uphold all of them concurrently.

When picking MLOps tools for your organization, a leader should consider:

Interoperability

More often than not, there will be some existing AI infrastructure already in place. To reduce friction in adopting a new tool, choose one that is interoperable with the existing ecosystem. On the production side, model services must work with DevOps tools already approved by IT (e.g., tools for logging, monitoring, governance). Ensure that new tools will work with the existing IT ecosystem or can be easily extended to provide this support. For organizations moving from on-premise infrastructure to the cloud, find tools that will work in a hybrid setting as cloud migration often takes multiple years.

Whether it's friendly for data science as well as IT

Tools to scale AI have three primary user groups: the data scientists who build models, the IT teams who maintain the AI Infrastructure and run AI models in production, and the governance teams who oversee the use of models in regulated scenarios.

Of these, data science and IT tend to have opposing needs. To enable data scientists to do their best work, a platform must get out of the way—offering them flexibility to use libraries of their choice and work independently without requiring constant IT or engineering support. On the other hand, IT needs a platform that imposes constraints and ensures that production deployments follow predefined and IT-approved paths. An ideal MLOps platform can do both. Frequently, this challenge is solved by picking one platform for the building of models and another platform for operationalizing them.

Collaboration

As described above, AI is a multistakeholder initiative. As a result, an MLOps tool must make it easy for data scientists to work with engineers and vice versa, and for both of these personas to work with governance and compliance. Knowledge sharing and ensuring business continuity in the face of employee churn are crucial. In AI product development, while the speed of collaboration between data science and IT determines speed to market, governance collaboration ensures that the product being built is one that *should be built at all*.

Governance

With AI and ML, governance becomes much more critical than in other applications. AI governance is not just limited to security or access control in an application. It is responsible for ensuring that an application is aligned with an organization's ethical code, that the application is not biased toward a protected group, and that decisions made by the AI application can be trusted. As a result, it becomes essential for any MLOps tool to bake in practices for responsible and ethical AI including capabilities like pre-launch checklists for responsible AI usage, model documentation, and governance workflows.

In the race to scale AI and realize more business value through predictive technology, leaders are always looking

Epilogue

for ways to get ahead of the pack. AI shortcuts like pre-trained models and licensed APIs can be valuable in their own right but scaling AI for maximum ROI demands that organizations focus on how they operationalize AI. The businesses with the best models or smartest data scientists aren't necessarily the ones who are going to come out on top; success will go to the companies that can implement and scale smartly to unlock the full potential of AI.

Manasi Vartak is the founder and CEO of Verta, an MLOps platform that enables data scientists and ML engineers to manage and operate AI-ML models at scale. She previously developed the open-source ModelDB model management system at MIT and worked on optimizing the news feed algorithms at Twitter and ad-targeting at Google.

APPENDIX

Case Study: Will a Bank's New Technology Help or Hurt Morale?

by Leonard A. Schlesinger

"If we grow too fast, we'll break from the strain."

"If we stop growing, we'll be eaten for lunch by our competitors."

Beth Daniels, the CEO of Michigan's Vanir Bancorp, sat silent as her chief human resources officer and chief

---

Adapted from an article in *Harvard Business Review*, July–August 2021 (product #R2104M). HBR's fictionalized case studies present problems faced by leaders in real companies and offer solutions from experts. This one is based on Leonard A. Schlesinger and Sarah L. Abbott, "Athena Bancorp," Case 919-517 (Boston: Harvard Business School, 2019).

Appendix

financial officer traded jabs. The trio had founded their community bank three years earlier with the mission of serving small-business owners, particularly those on the lower end of the credit spectrum. After getting a startup off the ground in a mature, heavily regulated industry, they were a tight-knit, battle-tested team. But the current meeting was turning into a civil war.

James Donnold, the CFO, had just presented an update on Vanir's aggressive goals: expanding to 15 branches, with loans and deposits increasing threefold in five years. Having already grown to five branches and $180 million in assets, the bank was right on track. But, James warned, competitors were circling, and Vanir needed to stay on the offensive. It couldn't let bigger banks lure away the previously underserved customers that it had brought into the financial system or let new "fintech" startups with digital-only banking services disintermediate its business. Luckily, James noted, the company's long-awaited new enterprise IT was nearly ready to go live, and it promised to greatly reduce the staff's workload—by, for example, using AI to automate tasks like calculating pricing and credit lines for customers.

That prediction prompted Mariko Wang, the CHRO, to let out an audible scoff. She felt that aggressive growth had already stretched Vanir too thin and that believing IT would lighten the burden on employees was optimistic. "When was the last time a new technology created *less* work for anyone?" she asked sarcastically.

But then her tone turned serious, and she delivered her familiar—compelling—spiel: Working with new or underserved banking customers was extremely arduous. Vanir's branches were open early and late to accommodate customers' schedules. To make banking less intimidating, tellers and relationship managers were told to take as long as needed to answer people's questions. They were trained to be unbiased, whereas some AI tools in the industry had come under criticism for discriminating against minority applicants. And that human touch was what drove growth; loan applicants often had such a great experience at Vanir that they transferred their other accounts to the bank, opened new ones, or recommended it to other small-business owners.

Vanir's associates enjoyed above-market salaries but also worked harder than their peers at other banks. Considered "essential workers," they'd even come in to the office during the worst months of the pandemic, managing all the loans that customers had applied for through the U.S. government's economic relief package. But now employee engagement was down, absenteeism was up, and customers were starting to notice. Net Promoter Scores had fallen, and comments in customer surveys included complaints like "hassled-looking teller" and "unhelpful manager."

"Our people are our strategy," Mariko said, locking eyes with Beth. "Without them happily serving customers, we're just another bank."

Off to See the Wizard

Leaving the meeting, Beth felt torn. She'd started Vanir to help hardworking customers who'd been neglected by large banks and poorly served by mismanaged community-development institutions. Her father had

Appendix

been a general contractor, and it infuriated her that the developers he worked for seemed to have unlimited access to debt while he struggled to secure a new loan to upgrade his tools and equipment. She suspected that most of the bigger players were interested in her customers only because they needed a certain number of small-business accounts to meet regulatory mandates and keep their banking charters; after luring small clients away with introductory promotions, the large banks would give them the same shoddy service that had held her father back. Meanwhile, the fintech startups were low touch and untested; they could leave their clients high and dry.

It hurt Beth's soul to imagine that possibility, so she shared James's fervor for quickly expanding to serve as many people as possible with the help of technology. The goal was to build a loan underwriting system that would apply proprietary algorithms to create a single score that signaled whether a loan should be approved and what the credit line and the interest rate should be. That promised to free up staff to focus on the face-to-face service that Vanir had become known for.

But building the enterprise IT had taken longer and cost more than anticipated. Meanwhile, associates had become accustomed to doing the calculations and decision-making themselves, and an inefficient process had become routine. The staff also enjoyed the autonomy the process provided: Lending officers were encouraged to get to know their applicants and to combine objective criteria, such as credit scores, with subjective ones, such as personal character. Still, the strain on the employees was starting to show, and Beth took Mariko's warnings about burnout seriously.

Would a shift to the new system help or hurt Vanir's staff? Certain elements of the transition would require lots of busywork. For instance, along with the lending algorithms, the IT team had built a customer relationship management system that would allow a review of customer profitability across multiple products. Information on that now was stored in loan officers' heads and hard drives, and getting it into the system would be laborious. As Vanir opened more branches, it would need to hire more associates, who would have to be trained (on, among other things, the new technology) by its existing staffers, further burdening them. Beth hoped that the new system's birth pains would be short-lived and quickly lead to greater efficiency and lighter workloads. But she also worried that in the long term, Vanir's earliest employees would miss the algorithm-free autonomy they'd become accustomed to.

Beth knew she needed to talk to "the wizard," her white-haired, tie-dyed-T-shirt-wearing chief technology officer, Bruce Richards. "What's the update?" she asked as she entered his office.

"Do you want the good news or the bad news?" he replied, chuckling. Beth frowned and crossed her arms.

"OK," Bruce continued. "The good news is that the entire stack is ready to go. We can roll out tomorrow."

"And the bad news?" Beth asked.

"The bad news is that the pilot we ran in the Lansing branch uncovered some, well, resistance."

Appendix

"Go on."

"The staff hated it," Bruce said. "The feedback was that no one had time to learn a complicated new system. Some people refused to attend the training. Others brought their laptops to class and worked the entire time."

"Oh," Beth said.

"This isn't unexpected!" Bruce interjected. "Learning a new system takes time and can be frustrating. You can expect a period of negative labor productivity before we see any gains, but that doesn't mean the gains won't come. What matters is that we're finally ready to launch. We can pull the trigger next week if you give us the go-ahead."

"No," Beth replied. "Hold off for now. We might have to delay. I need to think this through."

Some Frank Feedback

Beth checked her watch as she collected her coat from her office—8:30 p.m. So much for bankers' hours. As she headed out of the branch where the executive team worked, she saw relationship manager Chantelle Williams, one of her first hires, at her desk, turning over pages in a file. Beth knew that Chantelle had two sons who'd been homeschooling through most of the pandemic.

On Chantelle's desk was one photo of her kids and another of her first Vanir client—a bakery owner who'd had trouble obtaining a loan at other banks because of his prior issues with credit card debt. Following company protocol, Chantelle had looked more closely at his situation and realized that the debt had coincided with his wife's illness four years earlier. Since that time his credit history had been spotless. Vanir had given him a loan, and in return he not only made his monthly payments on time but accompanied them with deliveries of his delicious cannoli. "I don't stay late for you," Chantelle had once told Beth after she'd thanked the manager for her long hours. "I stay late to earn school tuition for them"—she nodded to the picture of her sons—"and," she added, shifting her gaze to the photo of the baker, "to make sure people like him can stay in business."

"How are you holding up, Chantelle?" Beth asked.

"I'm living the dream, boss!" Chantelle joked, gesturing to the open file on her desk.

"No, really. How's morale?"

"Well," Chantelle said, "a lot of people are struggling. You combine the long hours with challenges on the home front, and it's tough."

"I know," Beth said. "But I just spoke to Bruce Richards, and he said the tech solution is almost ready. Help is on the way."

Chantelle sighed.

"What is it?" Beth asked. "Are you worried about the transition? There will be some work up front, but I assure you that—"

"That's not what I'm worried about," Chantelle interrupted.

"Well, then, what?"

"Look, what makes this bank special is that we are run by people, not by formulas. We can make a human connection with our customers. I just don't think an algorithm can replace that. Truthfully, I'm worried that we're going to end up double-checking the algorithm all the time or, worse, that it will end up hurting our customers."

"Absolutely not," Beth said. "I wouldn't let that happen."

"You know how you call Bruce 'the wizard'?" Chantelle continued. "Well, have you actually looked behind the curtain? Are you sure this technology won't just end up discriminating against the very customers we strive to serve?"

After thanking Chantelle for her candor, Beth wished her a good night and headed for the exit. She knew she faced the biggest decision of her tenure as CEO. Should she rethink the implementation of Vanir's new IT system, knowing full well that her employees were stretched thin but that a delay might allow competitors to pounce on Vanir's current and future customer base? Or should she risk her employees' trust and dedication by pushing past their concerns, sticking to her tech-enabled strategy, and forging ahead? She opened the door and stepped out into the cold Detroit night.

The Experts Respond: Should Beth Go Ahead with the Bank's Expansion Plans and IT Rollout?

Bob Rivers is the chair and CEO of Eastern Bank

The bank's key differentiator is at risk. Beth should hit pause on the expansion. The clincher for me is that Vanir's Net Promoter Scores are falling. Superior customer service is the foundation of the bank's value proposition and the source of its competitive advantage. Beth should delay the enterprise IT rollout for at least a year.

The CFO is worried that this will provide an opening for fintech and large bank competitors. I don't agree. Big banks are built for efficiency, so they typically do very little handholding for small-business customers and transfer much of the paperwork to them through self-service. The fintech approach is even more extreme—a customer might never interact with another human. And Vanir's technology isn't what's most important, because it's not what its clients are buying. What they want is great personal service and advice, and small-business owners in particular will stay loyal to a bank that provides it. That's why Vanir must address the uptick in customer complaints before anything else.

How do you bring NPS numbers back up? Ultimately, Beth can take care of her customers by taking care of her staff. She's already paying above-market salaries, but that goes only so far. Even the most dedicated employees may decide that well-paying jobs aren't worth it if they're being overworked and can't see a light at the end of the tunnel.

So far, the bank's strategy of "character lending" and considering qualitative measures of creditworthiness has been successful. But many banks have taken a similar approach and failed, because human judgment isn't always reliable, and as a rule of thumb banks need more than 95% of their loans to be repaid to stay solvent. Beth seems to have found loan officers who can exercise their own judgment to make good loans. But I wonder how

Appendix

sustainable and scalable that is. We recently acquired a bank that made loans in a similar fashion—what senior executives described as "working in the comfortable shades of gray." That bank did this well, but it took more than 15 years for it to grow to $1 billion in assets. Vanir's growth plan is far more aggressive than that—so its risk profile concerns me. I also question whether its goals are even realistic. The algorithm-enhanced IT system might be a welcome addition to the process, but it should be implemented thoughtfully and carefully when employees are ready, not in a rush right now.

Although Vanir's CTO will be frustrated by a decision to halt the rollout, Beth can emphasize that she's not killing it, just delaying it until employees are less stretched and the NPS figures come back up. Yes, IT-enabled scale will eventually offer advantages to Vanir and help make it more sustainably profitable. But the bank can't relinquish what makes it competitive today.

Chris Yeh is a cofounder of Blitzscaling Ventures and the Blitzscaling Academy

Beth should move forward with the IT rollout and business expansion. A fledgling bank can't risk being outflanked by its competitors. She's understandably worried about the new algorithms and the stress that implementation will cause employees, but I think she can assuage their concerns with a more measured, inclusive approach and better messaging that emphasizes the system's augmented—rather than artificial—intelligence.

Vanir is at a pivotal moment. When a company starts out, its employees all know exactly what's going on because they're literally in the room when decisions are made. But this bank now has five branches and probably dozens of employees. Beth needs to change her management and communication strategy to handle the increased complexity.

First, there doesn't seem to be any consensus on the desirability of the new tech or who's in charge of rolling it out. James, the CFO, is an advocate but isn't involved, while Mariko, the CHRO, is against it but is probably overseeing the training for it. Bruce, the CTO, seems to have designed the system without adequately involving the loan officers and relationship managers who will use it. These are flashing red lights. When a project is this far along, the team should be on the same page about it, and each person's role should be clear and explicit.

The frontline workers who will use the system should have been consulted throughout, providing feedback to refine the product. Chantelle should not be worried that it will harm her connection with customers or be discriminatory.

Although competitive pressures call for Beth to implement the system, she needs to do so thoughtfully. She should characterize the launch as a beta release, slowly introducing the system in two branches and having employees work with the technology team to test and improve it. She should reassure staffers that it's meant to be a tool to make them better at their jobs, not to replace them or change the culture of the company.

At the same time, she needs to lift morale by being both a comforter and a commander in chief. It will take sincere public expressions of empathy and compassion—

Appendix

to the entire workforce and individual employees—to address the extreme toll taken by the pandemic. But Beth must rally the troops around the growth plans, too, because people also want to feel they're part of a winning team. She must explain that Vanir is currently in a sprint to ensure that it delivers on its promise of high-touch, technology-enhanced personal service even during the most trying of times.

The dynamic on her executive team also needs work. Her cofounders should not be sniping at each other. Disagreement is healthy; conflict isn't. Given the trio's history together, I suspect that the strain of operating during a pandemic is getting to them too. Beth should be up-front about addressing this with her executive team.

As Beth works to calm the current crisis and roll out the new tech, she must also undertake the harder and more important work of changing how she leads. I recommend that she start writing a weekly email to the entire staff or launch a private internal podcast with other team members so that people can get to know their coworkers, raise concerns, and perhaps most important, share stories that inspire them to keep going.

Leonard A. Schlesinger is a Baker Foundation Professor at Harvard Business School, where he serves as chair of its practice-based faculty.

Glossary of Key AI Terms

Algorithm. A sequence of instructions used to solve a problem, reach an outcome, or perform a computation. An algorithm can be simple, such as the recipe to bake a cake, or extremely complex, such as those that power internet search engines or self-driving cars. Algorithms may require human intervention to improve, or they may be machine learning algorithms that improve over time when they are trained with new data.

Analytics. The systematic computational analysis of data or statistics, used for the discovery, interpretation, and communication of meaningful patterns. Organizations may apply analytics to data to describe, predict, and improve performance. As analytics capabilities progress in an organization, they may go through stages of descriptive analytics (what happened), diagnostic analytics (why it happened), predictive analytics (what will happen), and prescriptive analytics (how to change what will happen).

Artificial intelligence (AI). The branch of computer science dealing with decision-making or prediction capabilities demonstrated by machines. In the business context, AI is usually supported by machine learning algorithms that make progressively better decisions or predictions over time.

Automation. The act or process of converting the controlling of a machine or device to a more automatic system, such as computer controls. Machine learning algorithms have vastly increased the number of cognitive tasks that can be automated.

Black box. A system whose inputs and outputs can be easily known, but whose internal workings are too complicated or hidden to be easily understood. An AI algorithm may have a black-box problem if its designers cannot determine why its output or prediction is unexpected, incorrect, or biased. An algorithm with a black-box problem might be described as lacking transparency or explainability.

Correlation. A measure of the statistical relationship between variables, indicating both the strength and direction of the relationship. Correlation is often confused with *causality*, the relationship between something that happens and the thing that causes it. For example, the appearance of umbrellas on a given day has a correlative relationship, but not a causal one, with raincoats.

Labeled data. Data provided to a machine learning algorithm with context or tagging. For example, a picture of a bird that is labeled "bird" or "animal" or "feather" or "wings."

Linear regression. A mathematical means of sorting out whether there's a relationship between two or more variables. It answers the questions: Which factors matter most? Which can we ignore? How do those factors interact with each other? And, how certain are we about all of these factors?

Machine learning (ML). A field concerned with the design and development of algorithms and techniques that allow computers to keep improving their performance over time without human intervention. The vast majority of AI in business is forms of machine learning.

MLOps (machine learning operations). A discipline that seeks to establish platforms and processes, and provides tools that make building, deploying, and maintaining AI systems faster, easier, and more reliable.

Natural language processing (NLP). A branch of AI focused on how computers can process language like humans do. Emerging business uses of NLP include speech recognition, language understanding, and language generation.

Overfitting. Overfitting occurs when a statistical model has too many parameters relative to the size of the sample. A model that suffers from overfitting may do a good job describing outcomes that already happened, but it won't predict future outcomes well. Overfitting is a risk if a machine learning algorithm is trained with poor or too little data.

Reinforcement learning. A branch of machine learning that optimizes tasks by learning from outcomes over time without requiring external training data. Applications of reinforcement learning include game-playing AIs, music or video recommendations, and optimized energy consumption.

Robotic process automation (RPA). RPA technology automates digital and physical tasks. RPA initiatives may or may not incorporate machine learning algorithms to improve over time. Uses of RPA include banking and finance process automation, data extraction, and customer care.

Supervised learning. A type of machine learning in which an algorithm is trained on *labeled* data. This requires the algorithm to learn from training data then apply learnings to new situations. Applications of supervised learning include stock price prediction, image classification, and facial recognition.

Training data. A data set (usually a very large one) that can be used to train a machine learning algorithm. The quality, amount, and in some cases recentness of your training data will affect a machine learning algorithm's ability to make better decisions or predictions.

Unlabeled data. Data provided to a machine learning algorithm without any context or tagging. For example, an image of a bird that is provided with no accompanying tag or text.

Unsupervised learning. A branch of machine learning that learns patterns from unlabeled data. Applications include targeted marketing, recommendation systems, and big-data visualization.

Index

academic approach, to risk mitigation, 157–158
Accenture, 124
accuracy rates, 76
administrative tasks, 2–3
Agrawal, Ajay, 79–87
AI. *See* artificial intelligence (AI)
AI agents, 103
AI assistants
  human traits in, 100
  onboarding of, 125–128
  training of, 99–100
AI Canvas, 80–87
Aida, 103–104, 106
Aiden, 209
AI operations team, 61–67
  in-house, 65–66
  third-party, 66
Airbnb, 168–173
AI systems
  data-centric approach to building, 40–43
  dependability of, 63
  employee embrace of, 117–122
  employee involvement in design of, 131, 133
  failures by, 147–151, 155–156
  feedback to, 132–133
  flexibility of, 64
  no-code platforms, 189–195
  production and deployment of, 39–40, 42, 43
  scalability and extendibility of, 64–65
  sustaining, 101–102
  training of, by humans, 99–100
Albert, 121
Alexa, 99
algorithms, 140
  biases in, 167–170
  consumer reaction to effects of, 172–173
  deployment of, 168
  detrimental effects of, 168–170
  market conditions and, 168, 170
  perception of, by targeted users, 170–172
  plan for faulty, 147–151
AlphaGo, 205–206
Amazon, 37, 126, 156
Amelia, 32
Amico, Richard, 1–7

Index

Ammanath, Beena, 179–186
amplification, of human capabilities, 102–103
Andreessen, Marc, 195
Apple, 102, 114–115
artificial intelligence (AI)
  See also machine learning
  adoption of, 37–40, 136–137
  case study of, 225–236
  human collaboration with, 97–116
  impact of, 97–98, 202–203
  implementation of, 125–137
  scaling, 217–224
  understanding, 33–34, 135–136
AT&T, 115
automation
  for micro-decisions, 140–141
  of processes, 208
  using AI, 98
automation projects
  case study, 92–93
  choosing, 89–94
AutoNLP, 200
autonomous systems, 140, 144, 145

Babic, Boris, 123–137
Baidu, 37
Beane, Matt, 133–134
biases, 15, 135
  in algorithms, 151, 155–156, 161, 167–170
  detection of, 161
  human, 25, 128–129, 132
  sources of, 185
big data, 17–18, 40–41, 48
black-box problem, 33, 100, 121, 136, 182–183

Blackman, Reid, 155–166, 179–186
Borealis AI, 209
business processes
  automation of, 27–29
  decision-making, 110–111
  flexibility of, 106–107
  personalization, 111, 114
  redesigning for collaborative intelligence, 98–116
  for reinforcement learning, 210–211
  scalability of, 108–109
  speed of, 107–108
business redesign, 104–114

Campbell, Craig, 80
capabilities, assessment of existing, 91
capability building, 90, 93
Carnival Corporation, 111, 114
causality, 19, 24
Center of Excellence (COE) model, 220–221
chatbots, 103, 106, 147–148
Chen, Daniel L., 123–137
classification, 74–75
clustering, 22
coachbots, 132–133, 135
cobots, 104, 106–107
cocreation, 105
Codex, 199, 201
cognition, theory of distributed, 134
cognitive engagement, 31–33
cognitive insight, 29–31
collaboration, 5–6, 223
collaborative intelligence, 97–116
collective intelligence, 134–136
company roles, 114–115

complexity, 22–23
compliance issues, 181, 182
confidence rates, 74
consumer internet companies, 37–40
consumer reactions, to AI algorithms, 172–173
control, loss of, 119, 130–131
corporate culture, 51
Cortana, 99, 103, 104
counterfactual explanations, 136
coupled systems, 134–135
creativity, 5, 102–103
credit approval, 101
credit card fraud, 107–108
cross-validation, 20, 23–24
customer interactions, 103–104
customer service, 31–33, 103–104
customization
    cost of, 39, 42
    human-machine collaboration for, 106–107

DALL·E 2, 199
Danks, David, 135
Danske Bank, 108
data
    analytics, 48–50, 53–59
    biased, 185
    big, 17–18, 40–41, 48
    bottlenecks, 63
    curation, 30
    enterprise data strategy, 93
    ethics, 155–166
    feedback, 85–86, 132–133
    high-quality, 41, 42
    image, 50
    input, 85
    for no-code platforms, 192–193
    overfitting, 22
    pattern detection in, 29–31
    personal, 102
    privacy of, 130, 133
    separating signal from noise in, 20–24
    small data sets, 38–39, 42
    sorting, 125–126
    text, 200–201
    training, 76, 85, 99–100
    use of, by AI, 14, 40–41
    visualization, 49
    wide, 18, 19, 25
data-centric AI development, 40–43
data compliance officers, 101
data governance board, 159–160
data science, 48, 49, 54
data science team, 47–52
data scientists, 33–34, 51, 53, 55, 71, 218, 222
Daugherty, Paul, 97–116
Davenport, Thomas H., 27–35, 55
decision-making
    analytics for, 49
    deep learning and, 33
    explanations for, 100–101, 136, 163, 182–183
    human, 3–4
    human in the loop (HITL), 141–142
    human in the loop for exceptions (HITLFE), 142–143
    human on the loop (HOTL), 143–144
    human out of the loop (HOOTL), 144
    micro-decisions, 139–145
    monitoring, 128–131
    prediction and, 18–19

Index

decision-making (*continued*)
  sequential, 206–207, 209–210
  in uncertainty, 80
  user modeling of, 126–127
  using AI, 79–87, 120–121
  using collaborative intelligence, 110–111
  using wide data, 19
decision-making tools, 139–145
deep learning, 30, 32, 33, 48, 50, 52
DeepMind, 199, 202, 205–206
design thinking, 5
digital twins, 110–111
discrimination, 173, 174, 182
  See also biases
distributed cognition, 134
Dreamcatcher AI, 102–103
Drucker, Peter, 131
dystopians, 112

efficiency, 12, 13
Elicit, 201–202
embodiment, of AI, 104
employees
  adoption of AI and, 117–122, 123–137
  decision-making by, 110–111
  fear of being replaced by AI, 123–124
  feedback for, 131–132
  impact of AI on morale of, 225–236
  incentivizing to identify AI ethical risks, 164
  negative impacts of AI on, 133–134
  new roles and skills for, 114–115
  resistance to change by, 119–120
employment opportunities, 101
endowment effect, 172
EQT Ventures, 4–5
Esposito, Mark, 61–67
ethical issues, 34, 101–102, 155–166, 223
  academic approach to, 157–158
  defining ethical AI standards, 182–183
  high-level AI ethics principles for, 159
  monitoring, 164–165
  "on-the-ground" approach to, 158
  operationalizing, 159–165
  organizational awareness of, 163–164
  risk mitigation for, 179–186
ethical risk framework, 160–161
ethics council, 160, 164
ethics managers, 101
Evgeniou, Theodoros, 123–137
exceptions, in decision-making, 142–143
exoskeletons, 104
expert systems, 33
explanations
  See also black-box problem
  for AI decisions, 100–101, 163, 182–183
  counterfactual, 136
  meaning of, 136
extended mind, 134

face recognition, 21
failures, 51
  cost of, 156–157
  ethical issues and, 155–157

plan for dealing with, 147–151
false negatives, 194
false positives, 194
Fast Forward Labs, 47
Fayard, Anne-Laure, 123–137
feature extraction, 20, 21–22
Feature Stores, 219
feedback data, 85–86, 132–133
foundational models, 199, 202–203
fraud detection, 107–108, 130, 194
Frick, Walter, 47–52
fusion skills, 114–115

game-playing systems, 205–206
Gans, Joshua, 79–87
gap analysis, 91
general artificial intelligence, 202–203
General Data Protection Regulation (GDPR), 100–101
General Electric, 110–111
Ghosh, Bhaskar, 89–94
GitHub, 199
Goh, Danny, 61–67
Goldfarb, Avi, 79–87
Goldman Sachs, 155, 156
Google, 37, 126, 156, 159, 199, 206, 209
governance teams, 159–160, 218, 222, 223
GPT-3, 198–199, 202
Gruetzemacher, Ross, 197–204

Harmer, Peter, 5
health care, ethics in, 161–162
health treatment recommendations, 31

hiring processes, 108–109
home security alarms, using AI Canvas for, 80–87
HSBC, 107–108
Hugging Face, 200
human autonomy, 130–133
human in the loop (HITL), 141–142
human in the loop for exceptions (HITLFE), 142–143
human judgment, 3–4, 25, 84
human learning, 14
human on the loop (HOTL), 143–144
human out of the loop (HOOTL), 144
humans
    as AI sustainers, 101–102
    assistance of machines by, 99–102
    collaboration between AI and, 97–116
    for explanations, 100–101
    machines assisting, 102–104, 124
Hume, Kathryn, 71–77, 205–213
Hutchins, Edwin, 134
Hyundai, 104

IBM, 155, 156
image data, 50
implementation phases, 125–137
    AI assistants, 125–128
    coach phase, 131–134
    monitor phase, 128–131
    teammate phase, 134–136
implicit bias, 185
informed consent, 162
InstructGPT, 198–199

Index

intelligence amplification, 141–142
intelligent agents, 31, 32
intelligent machines, as "colleagues," 4–5
interactions, 103–104
interoperability, 222
investment decisions, 132

job losses, 34, 112–113, 123–124, 133–134
job opportunities, 101
job replacement, 97–98
job skills, 114–115
judgmental bootstrapping, 126–127
judgment work, 3–4

Knickrehm, Mark, 115
knowledge work, automation of, 90
Koko, 100
Kolbjørnsrud, Vegard, 1–7

labor impacts, 97–98, 123–124
  of AI, 112–113, 123–124, 133–134
  of language-based AI, 201
language-based AI tools, 197–204
language models, 198–199
large language models, 198–199
lead scoring, 191
legacy industries, use of AI in, 37–40
legal decisions, 128–129, 167
legal issues, 181, 182

LIME, 183
linear regression, 73

machine learning
  See also artificial intelligence (AI)
  about, 12–13, 48
  AI and, 48–49
  algorithms, 72–74, 99–100
  applications of, 13–15, 18–20, 28–30, 32–33
  big data and, 18
  cross-validation and, 20, 23–24
  feature extraction and, 20, 21–22
  limitations of, 15–16
  mistakes to avoid using, 24–25
  opportunities to use, 71–77
  predictive analytics and, 55–59
  regularization and, 20, 22–23
  supervised, 20, 72–77, 207–208
  understanding, 13–16, 17–25, 33–34
  unsupervised, 22
machine learning operations (MLOps), 40–43, 218
  standardization of, 218–219
  teams for, 220–221
  tools for, 221–223
management, redefined, 1–7
management options, for microdecisions, 141–145
managers
  creativity needed by, 5
  decision-making by, 3–4
  knowledge of machine learning by, 17–25
  social skills of, 5–6

time spent on administrative tasks by, 2–3
Marble Bar Asset Management (MBAM), 126, 129, 132, 133
Martinho-Truswell, Emma, 11–16
Mason, Hilary, 47–52
maturity models, 90
Mayflower Autonomous Ship, 144
medical care prediction algorithm, 167–168
medical ethics, 161–162
medium-size businesses, AI for, 189–195
Mehta, Nitin, 167–177
Mercedes-Benz, 106–107
micro-decisions, 139–145
Microsoft, 147–148, 159, 199
Mizuno, Takaaki, 61–67
MLOps. *See* machine learning operations
Model Catalogs, 219
model-centric development, 40–41

NASA, 28–29
natural language processing (NLP), 126, 197–204
 applications of, 201–202
 capabilities of, 198–199
 preparing for future of, 200–203
Netflix, 126, 206
Ng, Andrew, 37–43, 72, 73
no-code platforms, 189–195

"on-the-ground" approach, to risk mitigation, 158

OpenAI, 198–199, 201, 202
operational redesign, 104–114
optimistic realists, 113
optimization, of processes, 208
Optum, 155, 156
organizational awareness, of ethical issues, 163–164
outcomes, of actions, 85
out-of-context model, 24–25
out-of-sample accuracy, 24–25
overfitting, 22

Pallail, Gayathri, 89–94
Pandora, 111
pattern detection, 29–31, 163
performance feedback, 131–132
personal data, 102
personalization, 111, 114
personalized recommendations, 19
pod model, 220–221
Power, Brad, 117–122
Prasad, Rajendra, 89–94
predictions, 18–19
 algorithms for, 73–74
 biases in, 167–168
 false results in, 194
 lowering cost of, 80
 testing accuracy of, 23–24
 using AI, 80–87, 207–208
predictive analytics, 53–59, 73
predictive models, 55
Predix application, 110–111
preferences, 19
privacy issues, 102, 130, 133, 135, 137, 161–162
problem solving, 11–12
 limitations of AI, 15
process automation, 27–29, 33, 208

Index

processes
See also business processes
  bespoke, 219
  for building and operationalizing AI models, 218–219
product data science, 49, 50
production environment, 62–65
productivity, 98, 113, 124
productivity skeptics, 113
product managers, ethical guidance for, 162–163
project opportunities
  automation projects, 89–94
  spotting, 71–77
projects, sequencing, 91
proof of concept, 39–40, 42, 43

racial disparities, 168–174
RAID (Research Analysis and Information Database), 126
reasoning capabilities, 128
recidivism prediction algorithm, 167
recommendation systems, 31, 49, 50, 125–126
regression analysis, 52
regularization, 20, 22–23
regulated industries, "black-box" issue in, 33
Reilly, Jonathon, 189–195
reinforcement learning, 205–213
  applications of, 206–207, 209–210
  capabilities of, 207–210
  opportunities for, 210–213
relationships, disruption of, 120
report writing, 3
research and development (R&D), 49, 51
resistance, to AI, 119–120, 123

risk framework, 160–161
risk mitigation, 157–165
  academic approach to, 157–158
  for ethical risks, 179–186
  in health care, 161–162
  high-level AI ethics principles for, 159
  "on-the-ground" approach to, 158
  technical tools for, 183–184
robotic process automation (RPA), 27–29, 33
robots, 104, 112
  accidents caused by, 148
Ronanki, Rajeev, 27–35
Ross, Michael, 139–145
Royal Bank of Canada, 209
rule-based expert systems, 33

safety engineers, 101
sales prospects, 191
scalability, 64–65, 108–109
scaling AI, 217–224
  standardization of model building and, 218–219
  teams for, 220–221
  tools for, 221–223
Schlesinger, Leonard A., 225–236
Schmidt, Eric, 203
search algorithms, 49
SEB, 32, 103–104, 106
Sedol, Lee, 205
selection, 23
self-determination, 161
self-driving cars, 121–122, 140, 182
sequential decision tasks, 206–207, 209–210
SHAP, 183

shrinkage, 23
Sidewalk Labs, 156–157
Siegel, Eric, 53–59
Singh, Param Vir, 167–177
singularity, 112–113
Siri, 99
small businesses, AI for, 189–195
smart-pricing algorithm, 168–173
social inequalities, 167–168
social skills, 5–6
software, 40, 48, 55–56, 126
    accidents, 148
    no-code platforms, 189–195
software-centric development, 40–43
software development, 201
software engineering, 50–51
spam filters, 49
speed, 107–108
Spotify, 206
Srinivasan, Kannan, 167–177
stakeholders
    engaging, in ethical issues, 164–165
    mobilization of, 121–122
    multiple, 223
standardization, of AI model building, 218–219
Starbucks, 111
statistics, 17, 19, 73, 74
supervised learning, 20, 72–77, 207–208
sustainers, 101–102
sympathy, 100

talent recruitment, 34
talent shortages, 39, 41
tasks
    administrative, 2–3
    automation of, 76–77
    breaking down, 75
    examination of, 75–76
Tay chatbot, 147–148
Taylor, James, 139–145
Taylor, Matthew E., 205–213
teams
    AI operations, 61–67
    assessing existing capabilities of, 91
    capability building of, 90, 93
    data science, 47–52, 220
    for ethics risk mitigation, 180–181
    governance, 159–160, 218, 222, 223
    for scaling AI, 220–221
technology optimists, 113
text analytics, 200
text data, 200–201
text summarization, 50
theory of distributed cognition, 134
Thomas, Robert J., 1–7
Thompson, Layne, 4
training, of machines by humans, 99–100
training data, 76, 85, 99–100
transparency, 136, 137, 172
trial and error, 208, 212
trust, 120–121, 135, 137, 174
Tse, Terence, 61–67

uncertainty, 51, 80
unconscious bias, 185
See also bias
understanding, trust and, 135
Unilever, 108–109
unsupervised learning, 22
user modeling, 126–127
utopians, 112

Index

Vanguard, 32
variables, 21–22
Vartak, Manasi, 217–224
Verneek, 201
virtual assistants, 103–104

Waymo, 121–122
wearable robotic devices, 104
West, Tessa, 131
wide data, 18, 19, 25
Wilson, Andrew, 124

Wilson, H. James, 97–116
work, future of, 112–113
worker displacement, 34, 112–113, 123–124, 133–134

Yampolskiy, Roman V., 147–151
Yeomans, Mike, 17–25

Zhang, Shunyuan, 167–177

Smart advice and inspiration from a source you trust.

If you enjoyed this book and want more comprehensive guidance on essential professional skills, turn to the HBR Guides Boxed Set. Packed with the practical advice you need to succeed, this seven-volume collection provides smart answers to your most pressing work challenges, from writing more effective emails and delivering persuasive presentations to setting priorities and managing up and across.

Harvard Business Review Guides

Available in paperback or ebook format. Plus, find downloadable tools and templates to help you get started.

- Better Business Writing
- Building Your Business Case
- Buying a Small Business
- Coaching Employees
- Delivering Effective Feedback
- Finance Basics for Managers
- Getting the Mentoring You Need
- Getting the Right Work Done
- Leading Teams
- Making Every Meeting Matter
- Managing Stress at Work
- Managing Up and Across
- Negotiating
- Office Politics
- Persuasive Presentations
- Project Management

HBR.ORG/GUIDES

Buy for your team, clients, or event.
Visit hbr.org/bulksales for quantity discount rates.

Notes

Notes

Notes

Notes

Notes